The
Pizza Express
Cook Book

The Pizza Express Cook Book

Peter Boizot

ELM TREE BOOKS / HAMISH HAMILTON
LONDON

To my mother, with love.

In writing this book I have been helped enormously by present and past members of PizzaExpress staff who are too numerous to mention individually but without whose application to making the company a success this book would never have been written.

I would also like to thank Mr Derek Miller of Queen Elizabeth College, the North American Pizza Association, Renée Brittan, Sarah Allen and Michael Danis for their help and suggestions. Roger Baker has helped immensely on the recipes whilst Lewis Winstock has been ever present to do research and give a helping hand.

Finally, a special note of thanks must go to Kate Dunning for her indefatigable and inspiring efforts to bring this book to fruition.

First published in Great Britain in 1976
by Elm Tree Books Ltd
90 Great Russell Street, London WC1

SBN 241 89196 5

Jacket design by the Bloomsbury Group, from an idea by Alan Aldridge
Photographs by Graeham French
Drawings by Enzo Apicella
Book design by Norman Reynolds

Filmset and printed in Great Britain by
BAS Printers Limited, Wallop, Hampshire

Contents

Note : In providing metric conversions for the recipes in this book, the aim has been to be as accurate as possible. One ounce equals 28.35 grammes ; by taking 28 grammes = 1 ounce as a basic conversion (instead of the frequently found 25 grammes = 1 ounce), the converted amounts adhere more closely to their true metric weight. This system also eliminates the necessity to make up for discrepancies as quantities increase. If a recipe calls for 112 g of an ingredient, the metric measurement can be doubled and still produce the right quantities.

Pizzajuolo

A Personal Pizza

THE FIRST TIME I heard the word *pizza* was, appropriately enough, in Italy. It was in Forte dei Marmi, not too far from Pisa, in 1948. I was staying with the Uzielli di Mari, a most civilised Florentine family, and good cooking was one of their many virtues. One sunny lunchtime we had a pizza. It was meant to be a treat and was introduced to the table with much laughter and excitement among the children. Apologies were offered—pizza could not be made as well in the north as in the south. But we all devoured it with pleasure. The dish made an immediate impact. It was colourful to look at, fragrant to smell, succulent to taste. I had stopped eating meat as a young boy, so the pizza's vegetarian nature also appealed to me. The pizza became, from that moment, a food which was to nurture my body and my pocket for many years to come.

Later, while I was doing National Service in Egypt, my delight in food generally and my budding romance with the pizza had both, necessarily, to be suspended. Later still, at university, food rationing continued so the fare was sparse and plain. For exotic tastes and new experiences, I had to rely on Indian or Greek restaurants. But in 1953, when fellow graduates were rushing into every conceivable sort of job brandishing their new degrees, I became a wanderer throughout Europe, on my way to see the world and incidentally taste its food.

I was part of that small group of nomadic exiles which in the mid-fifties had no collective name because it was ahead of the era of beatniks and hippies. We didn't wear beads or jeans or our hair long and most of us felt it was our duty to find a job. First of all I taught English in Paris where the rates of pay were low but the companionship of my fellow teachers excellent—and I don't think our results were bad either, judging from the way our European friends display their mastery of English when interviewed on television! In Paris, somewhat impecunious, I was pleased to discover at least a dozen inexpensive pizzerias and, inevitably, became addicted to a splendid bustling 'locale': in Rue St Benoit, a street in the heart of Saint-Germain-des-Prés. I noticed that an increasing number of pizzerias were springing up in Paris, presumably because standards of French *haute cuisine* were becoming more difficult to maintain, while pizza was relatively simple, inexpensive and profitable.

After Paris I went to the snows and chocolates of Switzerland, working for Nestlé in Vevey, where cheese fondue became my main gastronomic delight. Fondues and raclettes were not found so easily in restaurants in those days because, like pizza, their preparation took up a disproportionate amount of a busy chef's time—and they made the restaurants smell of cheese! In any case fondue was essentially a communal family event, prepared and cooked by the men in the home. Later, fondue became very popular commercially and increasing demand brought about great simplification of its preparation.

After my alpine adventures I took the road to Rome, virtually penniless but with just enough money to find lodgings in a room on the wrong side of the tracks which I shared with five Italian labourers—bricklayers, I think—who rose noisily at the crack of dawn while I slumbered on. Times were good then and money could be earned, so I was quickly able to fulfil one of my ambitions—to gourmandize my way around Rome's many pizzerias. I was working a split shift at the Associated Press, and in my time off I managed a barrow laden with tourist baubles such as postcards, views of Rome, earth from the Catacombs and other interesting, if dubious, souvenirs. I used horseshoes as paperweights to stop the postcards blowing away and one splendid day I sold one of these to an American tourist, who believed my tongue-in-cheek information that it came from Julius Caesar's horse! That incident started a completely new—and profitable—line. The Italian owner of my barrow almost wept for joy, saying it was pennies from heaven. The next day he appeared with a dozen rusty horseshoes threaded on a wire, begging me to sell them as well. The boys back home in Petticoat Lane would have been proud!

There was no time to eat during my busy days so by ten in the evening when I finished working, I was extremely hungry. No problem. Off I went to the nearest trattoria or pizzeria where I would polish off a litre and a half of wine with spaghetti or, more often, a pizza. Later on, in Germany, when I had more money to spend and perhaps even more energy to maintain, I would ignore the inevitable schnitzel and venison, and eat pizza *and* spaghetti—preceded, of course, by thick minestrone soup. When you are young and living it up you have no time to consider your waistline!

Oddly, perhaps, Germany was a great place for pizzas. Almost every town where Americans were stationed had an Italian-run pizzeria which became a haven for all foreigners who tired quickly of the repetitive and lengthy *gaststätte* menus. These were invariably cover-ups for schnitzel in one form or another and provided the customer with the same heavy and rather greasy food.

The most famous pizzeria was Mario's in Frankfurt's Kaiserstrasse. Mario originally opened this establishment as a restaurant with a string orchestra. Before long the musicians were gone, and their place was used for a pizza oven which was operated for many years by an adroit Neapolitan, Benito. I loved taking my friends there to watch Benito, in his blue and white striped shirt, throwing his pizzas high into the air—he was particularly adept at this and I can remember no occasion when he dropped one. Tossing pizza in the air is a great piece of theatre, which the customers love. It has an added value, too, as the centrifugal force helps to extend the dough in the gentlest way, and a trip through the smoky atmosphere does no harm to the flavour! In America they even have pizza flipping contests: the man who can toss a pizza and dance at the same time becomes a highly paid local hero.

Many excellent waiters and chefs began their careers in Mario's. He and his wife knew the secret of a good restaurant: be a real *patron*, run one place only, be there all the time, have your family help you run it. They chose their staff well, but woe betide any young waiter who was spotted taking it easy by the eagle-eyed Signora Mario, who was never afraid to hurl a few well-chosen Italian phrases when necessary. I sometimes wonder whether the clientele in restaurants would be so enchanted with the hustle and bustle if they could understand what the excited babble of the staff really meant.

Ultimately, however, the tiny Espresso Luna became my favourite pizzeria in Frankfurt. It was run – naturally enough – by another Neapolitan, Salvatore, and his family. The pizzas were always excellent and the juke box had a carefully selected variety of records which included classical, operatic and jazz music. This was later to become a pattern for the music in my restaurants, because a juke box allows such flexibility of mood in music – provided the right sort of records can be obtained. At the Luna, I particularly liked the scratchy *Valse Brillante* by Verdi, which I haven't come across since.

By now I had abandoned my barrow for a briefcase and my salesman's travels took me to many parts of Europe. I found pizzas in the most unlikely places, mainly where American Forces or oil men were living. Initially the pizzerias weren't frequented by the Germans or the French, but as time went by they became much more popular with the locals. Munich, Stuttgart, Paris, Nice and Cannes all had their pizzerias—as did many places which scarcely figured on the map.

I became quite an expert at eating pizzas, though not at making them. Undaunted, I was not beyond telling the *pizzaiolos* in Naples, of all places, that the edges of their pizzas were much too high and that if they wanted to please the visiting American sailors they should make the edges a bit lower! Eventually they got the message. I would also carry a few chilli peppers around in my wallet to liven up the pizzas in restaurants—usually Italian ones, believe it or not, which had not yet come across the American predilection for ever spicier pizzas.

3

I had, by this time, heard remarkable tales about the pizzas in America. Friends would throw their arms wide, saying 'They make them *this* big in New York.' In fact American pizzas proved disappointing the first time I tried them. So many things look 'real good' to the expatriates remembering them from a distance of 4000 miles. On subsequent visits to the States I discovered that you can find excellent pizzas there and I learned that it helps to eat them American-style, too—with your fingers!

It was ironic that of the cities I knew well in the 1960s, London was the only one where it was difficult to find a pizza worth the name. People would tell me that you could perhaps find a good pizza here, or there. Accordingly, I made special pilgrimages to this or that restaurant but seldom with any satisfaction. Eventually I was brought back to Soho, home of so much fine cooking. Here I ran into good pizzas at Otello's—which at that time was enjoying the huge success of being London's first trattoria—and at the Amalfi in Old Compton Street. The choice was limited, though, for the restaurants' main profits came from more expensive dishes. Their customers were intent on savouring the delights of spaghetti bolognese and vitello tonnato; only *cognoscenti* asked for pizza, and *good* pizza thrives best on continuous demand.

I visited many restaurants in search of pizzas, often accompanied by a fellow pizza addict and his long-suffering fiancée. Each time the pizza failed to appear on the menu, or to come up to expectations, I would stalk out muttering that the only thing to do was to set up my own pizzeria.

One evening, after we had been offered something that seemed to consist of three inches of dreary dough topped by a scraping of tacky cheese and a few sad olives, I had my usual grouse. My friend's fiancée, who may well have been slightly weary of these performances, seized her

4

chance. 'You are always talking about it,' she chided good-naturedly. 'For goodness sake, go and do it!'

So I did—and we both got married. In my case it was not to a lovely wife, but to a brand new business.

One evening, after eating a passable pizza at the Hosteria Romano in Dean Street, I complimented the *patron* but remarked that his pizzas were not really like those I had become used to in Italy and other countries on the Continent. It was, he explained sadly, impossible to cook them in England, or anywhere else, without a special oven. I asked why no one had ever imported such an oven from Italy. Someone had, he told me, but it had not been a success and the restaurant involved—the Romanella—was going into bankruptcy. He said that if I hurried I might just pick up that oven cheaply.

I didn't walk round to the Romanella. I ran, and begged the owner to let me see his oven. The next dawn found me gazing at this rare object as it stood forlorn, covered with a dirty tarpaulin, in a Pickfords' warehouse. It looked sad and old, and was beginning to rust. I couldn't imagine starting a multi-million dollar business with this, but even so, I put in an offer for £200. My generosity was not recognised, and the bid was rejected.

By now I had the bit firmly between my teeth and two days later I was in Rome on business, determined not to let the matter drop. 'Take me to your nearest pizzeria!' I commanded the taxi driver, who promptly dropped me off at a little place near the Stazioni Termini, doubtless musing on the habits of the mad English. The proprietor, who ran a take-away shop with a variety of pizza I had never come across before, sent me miles away to the outskirts of Rome where I found Signor Notaro, a manufacturer of pizza ovens. He acted as if he had been expecting me and soon convinced me that I was talking to a genius. Within minutes he was sketching plans for a most flamboyant pizzeria in London. After a short chat I paid him £600 for an oven. He promised to send it to England, together with a man to operate it. All I had to do was find somewhere to house it on arrival.

Back in London I began the arduous job of finding a site. There were few good pitches available and I had very little money indeed after I had paid for the oven and its transportation. As the essential cheese for pizza is mozzarella, and as already I felt I needed to tie up the manufacturer so that he could supply no other potential rival without first going through me, I contacted London's only mozzarella maker. This, by good fortune, led me to my first site. The cheese factory was owned by the charming Margaret Zampi, widow of the film director Mario Zampi and owner of the Romanella, that near-bankrupt restaurant whose oven I had tried to buy. Mario Zampi had written and directed a number of zany comedies including *The Naked Truth* and *Too Many Crooks* before his death in 1963. He had also had the vision of launching pizza in England on a grand scale. He had done the job properly, finding ideal premises in

Wardour Street, Soho, importing a special oven (which was electric as the authentic wood ovens were thought to be prohibited in our smokeless zones), and even setting up a factory to provide the best cheese. This was *fior di latte*—as near as he could come to true mozzarella in a country not blessed with wandering herds of buffalo. In 1959 he opened the Pizza-Express restaurant, hoping to entertain his movie stars there. Regrettably, they craved more luxurious food. Simple pizza was way ahead of its time and, thwarted, Zampi turned the PizzaExpress into an ultra-elegant restaurant.

Signora Zampi was most helpful and agreed to sell me all the shares of PizzaExpress Ltd which she owned. I bought them for £100 which I had borrowed from one of my oldest and best friends, Renée Brittan. Together with the company name, I took on the staggering task of repaying some £14,000 to the company's creditors. It seemed a lunatic deal, since I personally had never had the advantage of a solitary olive from these gentlemen.

On the bright side, I had acquired the Romanella, an endearing restaurant. It was one of the first to be designed by that master of the craft, Enzo Apicella. He had decorated it himself, with a little help from his artistic friends and a few crates of whisky. It was one of the earliest of a long line of restaurants designed by him. They were all cool, functional, noisy, somewhat anonymous yet friendly and full of individual touches, such as big leafy green plants and spotlights. It seemed a shame to cover his original murals of culinary scenes from Ancient Rome, but I decided there was no room for such decorative chic in what I intended to be a highly neon-lit, super hygienic pizzeria in a notably run-down street.

Armed with a sadly inefficient array of tools and paintbrushes but with the compensation of plenty of enthusiasm, my friend Poly, Earl of Norbury, and myself—with the help of stalwarts from the City—started to desecrate the interior of the Romanella. The bar proved particularly difficult and one morning we hailed three hefty passers-by to help us push over that strongly built shrine to Bacchus. We often wondered if the willing but puzzled fellows thought they were on 'Candid Camera'.

I was afraid that when my special oven—which weighed one ton—arrived from Rome it might just fall through the old Soho floor. We had a great game locating and fixing a steel beam to support the floorboards which we did with the help of a friendly Jamaican working on the Swiss Centre building site just across the road. When the oven arrived it didn't go through the floor—but then it wouldn't go through the door either! Ingeniously, we sent it quietly cruising around central London on its 40-foot-long low-loader while we set to and quickly knocked down one of the side walls, plate glass and all. As dusk fell, Poly arrived in his dinner jacket and, with more locals sharked up from the building site, stylishly supervised the unloading of the huge crate and its manhandling into my future restaurant. Then off he went—to a box at the opera, I suppose!

It was obvious that my intention was not properly understood by the denizens of Soho. After what seemed like months of hard work, the shop was still not open. One old gentleman strongly advised me to sell sandwiches in the street to cover my rent. Others, hearing that I was only going to sell pizzas and nothing else, clearly thought I was out of my mind. Hadn't Mr Forte tried it already and failed? An old friend of mine from Rome urged me to sell chips with the pizza. He was joking, I hope, as nothing could have been further from my mind. Perhaps my Roman adviser had accurately assessed English tastes, for three weeks before our own opening date, and to my utter anguish, a pizzeria suddenly opened right next door to us. And it offered side portions of chips! It was called the Dikko Bar and the proprietor used a cleverly thought-out American idea, baking frozen pizzas which were sold by the slice. I had the better site which, along with superior, hand-crafted pizza, helped me to beat his competition and subsequently buy him out. But we became the best of friends in the process, and Borge Ivanovic's name must go down as one of our pizza pioneers.

As my own venture slowly approached D-Day, a vast amount remained to be done. Before we even opened, my first manager, Gino Plato, left me. I had mistakenly thought he would help with the preliminary work and, in my optimism, had supposed that there would be very little for him to do. I was wrong. Crestfallen and apologetic, he told me that he was a professional restaurant man and scraping painted names off glass windows and the like was not his cup of espresso. I'm happy to say that Gino now runs one of the best Italian restaurants in London—the Imperia.

Gianni Giochi, my imported *pizzaiolo* who came with the oven, promptly announced that he, too, couldn't stay long. The fitting out was going ahead feverishly, with lots of help from my friends. There were home-made counters devised from dexion and hessian, hastily converted tables, do-it-yourself tiling with occasional bits of professional help whenever it could be found and afforded. It was looking rough and unready, but we had to open and open we did—on a Friday, 27 March 1965.

Gianni told me it was traditional to give away pizzas for the first few days and so like good junior *pizzaiolos* we followed the tradition. I suspect the reason the Italians do this is to test the oven and dough on the backs of the customers, but was surprised at the number of Sohoites who seemed to hold out three hands for free pizza and who wanted to take a piece for their brother as well. While pizza was free, we were busy; when we introduced our modest prices trade tapered off considerably.

Hours did not matter and at weekends we stayed open until four or five in the morning, with the juke box bellowing *O Sole Mio* or the latest Beatles' hit. The cosmopolitan population of Soho, from street brawlers to dukes, created almost a fairground atmosphere. Takings were never great because we only sold pizza at two bob a slice and had to sell an

enormous amount to make it worth while. Despite their good value, pizzas were slow to catch on.

Before Gianni returned to Rome he taught me how to make the dough and later I was helped with this daily task by a splendid grey-haired Sicilian lady, Gaetana, who worked for me during the first year or so, speaking little English but lending an authentic touch in her snowy white pinafore. Customers liked to watch her, standing next to the oven and always surrounded by sacks of flour, making the dough. We may not have known a lot about it in those days but at least people could see we were trying!

The Italian image was very prominent and deliberately cultivated. Few concessions were made to English nomenclature and our staff were mainly Italian—although later on we were to become like the League of Nations. I revelled in shouting around like a true Italian and few customers believed my Peterborough background. Without a little knowledge of Italian the enterprise would scarcely have succeeded, for how could *il capo* have communicated with his staff? Few of them spoke English. One night the Customs at Dover telephoned me to say that a Neapolitan, speaking no English at all, had arrived to work for me. 'Was this correct?' they asked, incredulously. He was listed as a plumber and they were about to return him to Italy. 'No, no,' I cried, 'he is here to make pizzas and, even if he is a plumber by trade, he is also a Neapolitan and all Neapolitans know about pizza, just as a Cockney from Bow knows about fish and chips.' They let him pass and Rino Silvestri became a star *pizzaiolo* and a highly successful manager.

The pizzeria I had set up on the advice of my Roman oven-maker, Signor Notaro, was based on a certain kind of Italian establishment known as a Pizza Rustica. In Rome these are as common as our fish and chip shops. Children even call in on their way to school in the mornings to collect a slab of pizza which they use to form a sandwich with a chocolate bar, Nutella, as a filling. Maids and millionaires go to work eating pizza in chunks, sometimes garnished with ham or salami. It is astonishing how so many Continental and American ideas do not catch on when they are introduced in this country; one thinks of bowling alleys, doughnut diners, delicatessens. The PizzaExpress was a different story. It did catch on, but not at first. And although it built up custom, its economic base held the seed of an early demise. With the high rents in the West End and our pizzas at giveaway prices, it could never have made enough money to survive.

I had intended to avoid the problems of washing up by serving slices of

---

PIZZ'A OTTE is an old Neapolitan tradition whereby the customer eats free at the opening of a new pizzeria by promising to pay in 8 days' time. When he returns to pay he has another free pizza, and so it goes on—an early form of Neapolitan American Express Card!

pizza on greaseproof paper; customers would eat standing up. That is how it works in the large, elegant bars of Rome and Milan and that's what I had hoped would happen here. But London isn't Italy and the English were not wise to pizza. I capitulated to my friends' advice and put in a few tables, but as I still wanted to avoid washing up, customers were served their slice of pizza on disposable plates and ate with plastic knives and forks. They drank their coffee from paper cups. This worked well except that when the piping hot pizza arrived the hungry customer often found his fork melting in the bubbling cheese!

By a stroke of luck I ran into an old college friend, Ronald Simson, who was to become the financial brain of the company. I don't think he was much impressed by the ramshackle appearance of PizzaExpress, or by its customers. The humble little tables had lost the grand damasks of the Romanella and were covered in fablon. Sitting there, watching half the great world of Soho drift by, was the other half. My inevitably amateurish work on the décor did nothing to overawe these *flâneurs* of Soho and they hung around in alarming numbers, sitting long and spending little.

Wisely, Ron Simson suggested we should start to trade up a little and soon we were serving pizza on best Woolworth china. Takings started to climb, but the going was still tough and I had many an eyeball to eyeball confrontation with creditors who still harboured their doubts. I promised to pay them all if they would only give me time to make some money. The patient ones kept my account for years and saw it grow, though I suspect they viewed the lengthening line of credit, which helped us to open more branches, with mixed feelings.

Somehow we prospered. We paid off our debts. Two years later we opened a second establishment in Bloomsbury. This branch, in Coptic Street, was an instant success and I regard it as one of Enzo Apicella's masterpieces. Originally it was an old Express Dairy, tiled and cool and with charming decoration. Enzo knew, intuitively, exactly what to leave and what to add. I was unable to find out the overall plan in advance and my friends were dismayed by the lack of drawings. I would dutifully press Enzo for more details, but he said, and I knew, that it would be all right. When pressed, his Neapolitan hackles rose. He ranted, he crooned, he said not to worry: a squiggle here—waving his hand; a touch of green there—pointing to the ceiling; a man to make Neapolitan-style pizzeria lamps, another to make a Neapolitan-style counter, another to paint the place in colours which didn't really exist and *Gesu Christo!*—it would be perfect! I had to promise Enzo a big opening party; that, plus faith in him, was all he asked of me.

The result was highly successful. We had a party, which would not have disgraced Rio at carnival time, and Enzo's excellent design won high praise. Coptic Street thrived because it was beautiful and because it was in a gastronomic desert where we had a hungry flock of local professional people and visitors to the British Museum.

It was in Coptic Street that the Original String Quartet first started to play in public; they have now become a tradition—in addition to establishing a nationwide reputation—and still play there regularly. It is our most successful branch thanks to the capable management of Frenchman Patrice Brun, who like so many in our company started at PizzaExpress as a *plongeur*.

The next link in the pizza necklace—I don't like to think of it as a chain—was a corner site in Fulham Road, beneath Mary Quant's old workrooms. It was a success from the start. Yet another Enzo masterpiece—simple, unified and pop for a change. To maintain the integrity of the fascia design, which was not accepted by the Chelsea Council, I had to appeal to the Minister of Town and Country Planning, armed with a 300-signature petition from my customers. He consented to the PizzaPizzaPizzaPizzaPizzaPizza sign in blue neon which goes so stylishly around the sides of the restaurant, and which Enzo had steadfastly refused to alter. It became our unofficial badge and nickname of the company—PizzaPizza.

The next property Ron Simson and I acquired was the Golden Age of Gingerbread in London's Notting Hill Gate. Eventually its name was changed to PizzaExpress, but not before its fascia inspired Gingerbread, the organisation for single parents. Then a former cinema in Hampstead was added to the company, and is now a delightful pizzeria with an outdoor garden. A second outlet in Soho was born when Moka Ris, one of the earliest homes of expresso, became a PizzaExpress. At this Dean Street site we took into partnership out longest established manager, Mario Molino from Naples, who later became the first PizzaExpress franchisee when he opened his branch in Gloucester Road, Kensington.

We ventured across the river with a second franchise in Wimbledon and a branch in Streatham, locations rather different from our traditional sites in the West End and the bed-sitter belt, then over the sea to Jersey. One hopes the story has not ended there, and that our expansion will continue, primarily through franchises. We have also cast our eyes towards Europe. Evidently the formula works well there, too, for it was imitated down to its very last detail by one of our ex-waiters who opened a replica of PizzaExpress in Athens. He pirated our designs for menus, business cards, sugar sachets and of course our way of making pizzas. The Greeks eat a Four Seasons, suitably translated, seated on red kitchen chairs in front of red-legged marble-topped tables, surrounded by designs on the wall straight from our Chelsea pizzeria. Copyright is difficult to enforce in Greece and of course our Greek imitator receives none of the help from the mother company which a franchisee would receive in this country. Perhaps we shall one day see a pizza with vine leaves!

One of the reasons that PizzaExpress has achieved its modest success is because we have always striven to be authentically Italian—not easy when one is removed from that country by some 1000 miles. We have encouraged Italian staff, used Italian ingredients and equipment, and looked mainly to Italy for our inspiration. In recent years it has become increasingly difficult to find Italian workers, and we now have many Spaniards, North Africans, South Americans and other nationalities who work hard and well in the Italian tradition.

Another reason for our success is, I am sure, our willingness to compromise and be flexible but not to surrender. In the fast food business it is easy to serve plastic food in a plastic environment, to put undue emphasis on low cost ingredients, and to become a slave to the annual accounts. I never will. I shall remain dedicated to quality and authenticity, preferring to maintain a decent standard, and knowing that there are always at least ten pizzerias in London where I can find good food in agreeable surroundings.

A Historical Pizza

AFTER ONE OF his rapturously received performances at the Metropolitan Opera in New York, the great tenor Enrico Caruso was asked for his secret: how did he control such power and passion, and project such lush sweeps of melody? Looking his questioner straight in the eye he replied: '*E la pizza, la pizza, caro mio!*' And no doubt proceeded to cut into yet another slice of the classic Napoletana.

Caruso was paying unusual tribute to a great national dish of his own country which was not particularly well known outside Italy at that time—except, as it happened, in New York itself where Italian immigrants had introduced the tradition of the pizza. It is almost a hundred years since the pizza became an integral part of the cross-fertilization of American society. The British, naturally enough, were a bit disdainful of pizza, travellers and cooks alike ignoring it, or referring to it as a curiosity.

The street criers of old Naples were surely the first to sing the praises of *la bella pizza* for it is with that city the pizza is most closely associated, although its origins recede into the mists of antiquity. In its simplest form, the pizza could have been invented by the Phoenicians, the Greeks or the Romans; anyone, in fact, who learned the secret of mixing flour with water and heating it on a hot stone.

Our knowledge of Roman cookery derives mainly from the excavations at Pompeii and from the great cookery book of Apicius. This includes recipes which involve putting a variety of ingredients on a base of bread: he uses chicken meat, pine kernels, cheese, garlic, mint, pepper and oil—all ingredients of the contemporary pizza—arranged in a hollowed-out loaf. He concludes with the instruction '*insuper nive, et inferes*'. Which means 'cool in snow, and serve'! The result would be something between a smorgasbrød and a sandwich. There is no real evidence from classical times of pizzas as we know them today, though Pompeii has shops, complete with marble slabs, cans, and other tools of the trade,

13

which resemble the conventional pizzeria. The Museo Nazionale at Naples exhibits a statue from Pompeii which because of its stance is called *Il pizzaiolo*, but the label is an imaginative one.

It is clear that one cannot define any simple genealogy for the pizza. Probably every ancient culture that evolved a form of bread quite quickly decided that it was less dull if something was put on to it, and what emerged was characteristic of that culture. The Mexican tortilla, Indian chapati, Scottish bannock and Greek pitta are just a few varieties of milled cereal in flattened form; none of them is specifically related to pizza. However, the Italian Historical Association of America finds a connection between pizza and matzo, the unleavened Passover bread of the Israelites. The Normans baked something called a trencher, a flat loaf on which they served their food. After they had eaten what was on top of the bread, they polished off the trencher itself. And Katie Stewart has a traditional Middle Eastern recipe for dough discs topped with a fragrant meat sauce, which are eaten folded in the hand—certainly very similar to the pizza in style. The recipe is interesting because the filling is cooked with the bread, and this is also the special characteristic of the pizza. Instead of introducing the already cooked filling to the separately prepared bread (kebab in pitta, for instance), the pizza blends both in a distinctive aromatic whole.

There have, however, been some imaginative speculations about the legendary origins of the pizza. Two American pizza hierarchs, Larry Goldberg and Mike Losurdo, think that Roman Legionnaires baked pizzas on their shields after fermenting the dough in their helmets on long route marches under the burning sun. Larry, who has been crowned Pizza King of New York by *New York* magazine, even traces the history back to the soldiers of Darius, King of Persia. No doubt the troops sliced up the mozzarella with their swords, too!

Mike Losurdo also quotes the fable that the dish was invented for a twelfth-century nobleman by a chef named Pizza, which is surely as apocryphal as the story that it originated in a town called Pizza.

The very word itself seems to have come from nowhere. It is vernacular for pie in Italy, yet does not appear in some of the weightier Italian dictionaries to be found in the British Museum.

But speculation about the distant antecedents of the pizza is little more than a pastime, for today the authentic pizza is associated with tomato; in fact a pizza without its tomato base is unthinkable to most people. Although the tomato was introduced to Europe as early as the mid-sixteenth century, it was another two hundred years before the fruit was cultivated as a foodstuff.

The Italians adored this new fruit, which they called the *pomo d'oro*, or golden apple. Today it is virtually impossible to imagine Italian food without the tomato. The wary British took much longer to appreciate the fruit and were shocked by the way in which Italians and Spaniards cooked and ate it. As late as 1850 the British still believed that the golden apple (though by this time tomatoes were red) caused gout and cancer, which may be one reason why Italian cooking generally, and pizza in particular, did not become popular here as it did in America.

In *French Provincial Cooking*, Elizabeth David writes about the Provençal onion pie called *pissaladière*, which is a form of pizza with onions, tomatoes, anchovy fillets and olives on a yeast pastry. The accent is on the onions and Mrs David speculates that this was originally the Roman proto-pizza, without tomatoes, introduced to France by the cooks of Rome during the fourteenth-century sojourn of the Popes in Avignon. This suggests that a pizza like the one we enjoy today, but without tomato, may have been known before that fruit was established in Italy.

It is unlikely that pizza just arrived through a brainstorm of genius—as Charles Lamb would have us believe that Bo Bo lighted on the glories of roast pork. It is more likely the end product of trial and error by swarms of Neapolitan cooks.

In sixteenth-century Naples, the tavern of Cerriglio was famous, and there the Spanish soldiers of the Viceroy devoured proto-pizza with appetites worthy of Pantagruel. Although pizza is traditionally the food of the taverns and the little streets, there is no trace of it in early popular lore. Paradoxically, we know most about the popularity of the pizza through its connection with captains and kings.

Ferdinando IV of Naples (1751–1821), the first king of the Two Sicilies, put a pizza oven into the kitchens of the royal palace of Capodimonte to satisfy the whim of his wife, Queen Maria Carolina, who must have been among the first celebrated pizza addicts. After the unification of Italy, Queen Margherita, wife of Umberto I, went one better when she visited Naples in 1889.

The royal couple were Piedmontese and had become over-familiar with the usual international cuisine, the nineteenth-century equivalent of jet-set Hilton fare. In Naples they asked for something different, a local speciality perhaps. As a result, a messenger from the Palace of Capodimonte appeared at one of the oldest pizzerias in Naples, the Pizzeria Brandi. It still exists today, and the owner will proudly show you a piece of marble from the original fascia. In the 1880s, the establishment was run by Raffaele Esposito who had taken over from the celebrated Don Pietro Colicchio, the first Pizza Pete on record. He was the professional par excellence and when he died they found him slumped against his oven holding a still-hot pizza. Pietro was so well known that Raffaele, his successor, was also known as *Pietro il pizzaiolo*.

So off went Raffaele alias Pietro and his wife, to prepare pizzas to royal command. They cooked three varieties which delighted the king and queen, but the monarchs were particularly taken with one which Raffaele devised especially for the occasion with a splendid combination of culinary style and diplomatic courtesy. It was delicious, delicately seasoned and had the tenderest edge. In honour of his sovereign, Don Raffaele had created a pizza in the colours of the new Italian flag: there was the red of tomatoes, the green of basil and the white of mozzarella cheese.

The queen responded majestically to the compliment and wrote a letter of praise to the *pizzaiolo*. The Margherita was born! Every time the royal couple were in Naples, Raffaele and his wife would be summoned to prepare the food. Today the Margherita is an international classic, one of the best. Don Raffaele achieved further fame, for it was reputedly he who first combined mussels, mushrooms and anchovies with mozzarella for a pizza topping.

Although the Italian royal family was busy taking the pizza to its heart, the English remained unimpressed. The first Englishman to name pizza was probably W. J. A. Stamer, who wrote *Dolce Napoli* in 1878:

> *O capito, O capito*. No need to bawl yourself hoarse, my friend; your merchandise requires no chanting; nor yours either, *O Pizzaiolo*; it speaks for itself. *Pizza maladetta!* Had thy originator

choked himself with the first mouthful he ate of thee, none, save the members of the medical profession, would have reason to mourn his fate. Pizza, dearest of all comestibles to the Neapolitan palate, much hast thou to answer for; indigestion art thou in its compactest, deadliest form. It required not the creative powers of a Caramel to bring thee into existence: Mother Eve might have conceived thee, or Sarai. Take of dough as much as is sufficient unto thee, and to the thickness of thy thumb with thy hands flatten it; anoint profusely with oil of olive, and dab in pieces of garlic, anchovy, strong cheese, rancid bacon, and whatsoever else may be highest in flavour and lowest in price; put into a hot oven, bake, and thou hast a pizza. Eat thereof hastily and repent at leisure.

It may seem that with friends like Mr Stamer, the pizza needed no detractors, and when W. G. Wates described 200 Italian recipes in *The Cook's Decameron* (1901) pizza didn't get a single mention. Two years later *The Gourmet's Guide to Europe,* compiled by Lt-Col. Newnham Davis and the piquantly named Algernon Bastard, dismissed *Pizza alla Pizzaiolo* as 'a kind of Yorkshire Pudding eaten with either cheese or anchovies and tomatoes flavoured with thyme.' It may be as well to remember that English travellers abroad tended to remain rather insular in their attitudes and were notoriously vague about foreign ingredients. They were, for example, always confusing aubergines with courgettes, and Lt-Col. Davis probably thought oregano was thyme. Also, they may have eaten pizzas cooked in inferior kitchens just as today English fish and chips can be delicious or soggy and greasy according to the shop you choose. Yet beautiful pizzas, besides the Margherita, were being developed at this time, including the classic Pizza all'Andrea—named after the famous Italian Admiral, Andrea Doria—with its black olives, tomatoes and anchovies. What certainly emerges is that pizza was often a street food, quickly put together, highly flavoured but variable in quality. Folded in two and then in two again, like a book, it was, as it still is, eaten *al libretto* by people in a hurry.

It seemed that the pizza was, in company with other regional delicacies like Yorkshire Pudding and 1,000 Year Old Eggs, destined not to travel. Until, that is, it found its way across the Atlantic with the Italian immigrants. The first American pizzeria opened in New York around 1895 and Gennaro Lombardo, who went into business a few years later, is now known as America's *Patriarca della Pizza*. From New York, where the old Italian community still refers to a pizza as 't'mater pie', the pizza rolled westward. It was introduced to Chicago by a pedlar who walked up and down Taylor Street with a metal wash-tub of pizzas on his head, crying his wares at two cents a chew. It's difficult to believe he was anything but an Italian, and he must have been a traditional *pizzaiolo,* because this is the way pizza used to be sold in Naples, in copper cylindrical drums with false bottoms which were packed with charcoal

from the oven to keep the pizzas hot. The name of the pizzeria was embossed on the drum.

Pizza's popularity grew steadily throughout the first half of this century, but it was not until the 1950s or 1960s that America really sat up and noticed. Celebrities of Italian origin such as comedian Jerry Colonna, Frank Sinatra, Jimmy Durante, and baseball star Joe DiMaggio all devoured pizzas and the public followed their lead. Some pizzaiologists say it wasn't an Italian-American but James Dean who gave the pie its real boost. Others have joked that it was Dean Martin's line which set America salivating: 'When the moon hits your eye like a big pizza pie, that's *amore*.' Whatever the reason, Dale Brown, writing in 1969 about American food, could say: 'The pizza continues its boom. Few roads leading into our cities are not now perfumed by the warm odour of tomato, cheese and oregano; and the pie small, medium or large has wheeled out on to the superhighways in its conquest of America.'

Inevitably, it was in America that the world's first Pizza Trade Association was formed. It happened in 1968 in Ypsilanti, Michigan, where the Midwest Pizza Association—subsequently to become the North American Pizza Association—raised the flag. NAPA's journal, *A Slice of Pizza*, was soon reflecting the highly competitive, efficient and ebullient American attitudes to business. Besides being crammed with marketing and product information, it contained a good leavening of lighter material—introductions to fast-baking, quick-selling Pizzamen (and Pizzamates too). There were also occasional horrendous stories about pizza-eating competitions and giant pizzas. It was NAPA which helped *The Guinness Book of Records* to track down the world's largest pizza. The statistic has only recently changed: a pizza 21 feet in diameter and weighing 1,000 pounds, baked by Pizza Pete at South Pulaski Road, Chicago, on 3 May 1970 has been eclipsed by a 30-foot 10-inch pie weighing 1,058½ pounds, which was sold in 6,000 slices in Cliftonville, Ohio, on 4 July 1974.

Another useful and interesting function of NAPA is 'pizzacation' of the public, which means publicising all the good things about pizza. Other schemes launched by these aggressive pizzateers include marketing slogans galore: 'Hurry back! We knead the dough!'; 'Seven days without a pizza makes one weak.' In a more serious vein NAPA can be a staunch defender of the product. When an Alka Seltzer TV commercial seemed to knock pizza as indigestible NAPA arose in wrath, and hammered the offending pharmaceutical company into apology.

One hopes the pizza will achieve comparable national status in this country and inspire as powerful a trade association, for during the last decade it has become part of our national eating habits. The young especially have taken to it, but it is essentially a taste that transcends age and class. Unlike many inexpensive foods the pizza is not a poor man's substitute for something else, whatever it may have been in the alleys of old Naples. Quite the opposite, in fact, for a pizza offers excellent food value. The American pizza recipe on page 50 contains ingredients from four basic food groups—cereals, dairy products, vegetables and meat. Tests carried out by the Department of Nutrition at Queen Elizabeth College, University of London, show that the Margherita recipe on page 43 contains 750 calories using the same basic dough and 950 calories using the enriched dough. The recommended daily intake for a moderately active male aged 18–35 is 3,000 calories. A nine-year-old girl requires 2,300 calories a day; a nine-year-old boy needs 2,500. This means that a pizza contributes significantly to our calorific requirements but is not overloaded with calories to cause obesity. It can even be used in a slimming diet, because it contains a normal amount of carbohydrates (57%) in relation to calories. A Margherita made with the basic dough recipe provides one-third of the protein, 99% of the calcium, 25% of the iron, 26% of the thiamin (B_1), 43% of the riboflavin (B_2), 44% of the niacin, 41% of the vitamin A, and 23% of the vitamin C suggested as the recommended daily intake for a moderately active male between 18 and 35. When it is remembered that the Margherita is one of the simplest recipes it can be seen just how nutritious pizza is; and the many additions possible on a pizza will only increase the waistline when the weightier ingredients are used. With a green salad as a side dish and a fruit salad to follow, the pizza makes an extremely nourishing and complete meal.

I may be biased but I think, too, that the lusty scent of a pizzeria is so much more delightful, aromatic and nostalgic than those of restaurants dealing with other—usually fried—forms of fast food.

I have heard it said that the older a civilisation becomes the more its taste requires sharp flavours. We see this with the Chinese, Egyptian, Indian and Mexican cuisines. As our civilisation rolls on into the twenty-first century and our economy becomes less lavish, our tastes too are becoming more accustomed to spicier foods. The age of oysters and caviar may be on the wane, but the future looks golden for the inexpensive, mouthwatering pizza.

Pizza Dough

M AKING A PIZZA from basic ingredients is a very satisfying piece of creative cooking. And it isn't too difficult. The base, the transformation of flour and water into a soft, malleable doughball by honest and hearty kneading, always gives me a real sense of achievement.

Many people are nervous of working with yeast, but such fears are unfounded if you follow the simple instructions (pp. 25–29). True, it can be a slightly messy or sticky business at first because you are, after all, working with a natural glue—flour and water. But as the Italians say, '*Non si lavora in un molino senza infarinarsi*' which means, more or less, that you don't work in a flour mill without getting flour in your ears.

Flour

Use ordinary, plain flour, preferably not too strong. Strength of flour is measured by the protein count and at PizzaExpress we use one which is 12 per cent. I have brought back to England samples of flour from some of the oldest Italian pizzerias—such as the Pizzeria Port'Alba, founded in 1830, where Luciano Vincenzo still makes his famous dough by hand in a kind of wooden trough, as Neapolitans did for centuries before electricity came along—and have had them tested by the Flour Milling and Baking Research Association. These tests showed that a weak flour is frequently used, as little as 8.5 per cent (standard Italian '00' grade flour is 10 per cent). A very strong flour will make the finished dough difficult to stretch when you put it into the pizza pan, unless you add a dough extender such as soya flour which renders it more supple. I have tested most of the flours easily available on the supermarket shelves and found that they are all capable of making a very adequate pizza dough. Wholemeal flour can be used for a 'brown' pizza, of course, and I have included two recipes using self-raising flour for a palatable quick pizza. But the authentic flavour and feel comes from the combination of plain flour and yeast.

Make sure that the flour is reasonably warm when you use it; in fact, it is best if all the ingredients used in making dough, along with the equipment, are at a temperature of around 27°C (80°F). If your flour barrel sits in a cool larder, bring out the quantity you need in plenty of time so that, like a good claret, it can become *chambré* before you use it.

In post-war Italy some pizzerias once used what can only be described as 'hot' flour, because originally it had been sent by the American people as a gift to the Pope! How this generous offering finished up on the marble counters of back street Roman pizzerias is not for me to say. But it did produce exceptionally mouth-watering pizzas, which were often unwittingly eaten by those Americans who had sent it over in the first place as a charitable donation.

Always sift the flour before using it. Flour sifters date from the time when flour was sold including the occasional impurity or foreign body. This doesn't happen today with the products of modern mills, of course, and flour is much finer now anyway. But the sifting distributes air and you are already on your way to producing a light dough.

Salt

This is very important. It is so easy to forget to put salt in the dough that even some large plant bakeries have electronic salt detectors, because the professionals, too, have bad memories. I suggest that you put the amount of salt you need on to the flour as you measure it on the scales, and sift them together. Too much salt will kill the yeast, but leave it out and the dough will be flavourless.

Yeast

Fresh yeast and dried yeast are equally suitable for making pizza dough. Probably because it is a living substance, fresh yeast seems to me to have much more character to it. An ounce or so of its creamy nature will do wonders for your health. 'Two penn'orth of yeast from the baker's does you the world of good,' my grandfather used to say—and he died with his boots on, working as ever, at 89. It is certainly rich in Vitamin B.

Yeast needs warmth and moisture to grow and is affected by extremes of temperature. While strong heat will kill it, extreme cold will not; it will merely retard its growth. This explains why dough can be stored before the rising process in the refrigerator, or deep frozen for a long period. Sugar helps yeast to grow, but salt, again, checks its progress—so don't be tempted to dissolve the salt in the water with the yeast when making the yeast liquid.

Fresh yeast is remarkably inexpensive and, as health food shops proliferate, is once more easily available throughout the country. Your local baker will usually sell you an ounce or two. If you have to buy as much as a quarter pound (yeast is very light compared with its bulk), I suggest you cut it into one-ounce pieces and freeze it. It will stay good for many months; English yeast is exported all over the world in a frozen state. Unfrozen, fresh yeast will keep in the refrigerator for four or five days, provided it is covered.

Dried yeast is much more readily available and can be found in most big supermarkets and chemists, put up into small drums or sachets. It will keep, in a cool place, for about six months or longer. Generally, half the quantity of dried yeast to fresh yeast is a good guide, but it is essential to read the instructions on the tin or packet, since brands vary a little.

Yeast should always be dissolved in a little tepid water before being incorporated into the flour. Crumble fresh yeast with your fingers, stir dried yeast with a fork. Add a little sugar to the warm water to help the yeast to grow. The addition of sugar also helps the pizza to attain a rich, golden colour.

Water

The Neapolitans, and even the jealous Romans, will say that the reason you find the best pizzas in Naples is the quality of the water. In the old days the water for Naples came from the Springs of Serino, near Avellino, and was, indeed, exceptionally pure. Today the town has outgrown the supply from Serino and uses a more mundane source, but this water still makes some of the best coffee, beer and, of course, pizzas in the whole of Italy.

While preparing this book, I carefully smuggled back to England some water from a Neapolitan pizzeria and had it analysed. It revealed no special qualities which would account for the secret of fine pizza. And judges of baking competitions in England tell me they do not consider water to be a particularly important factor in producing fine dough. Otherwise, they point out, entrants from the same region would keep winning the prizes, and this does not happen.

You may find you make a better dough if you boil the water before using it. This is a secret passed on to me by an old *pizzaiolo* from Naples who, perhaps fearing retribution from the gods for giving the game away, asked that his name should not be mentioned. Perhaps there *is* some magical quality about the water in Naples, but don't drink it more than a yard off the coast!

Equipment

It is a case of 'clear the decks' when you are going to make a pizza, and the more uncluttered space you can give yourself to work on, the better. Cool marble is the best working surface, but formica and enamel are almost as good. If you don't have a lot of space and plan to make a slew of pizzas, you will find that more mixing bowls will come in handy, as they can hold or cover the doughballs when you have made them.

The baking trays or pans are important. Neapolitan *pizzaiolos*, of course, do not use them, and you can try to copy them if you wish. You will need, though, a large peel, or paddle, to slide the pizza in and out of the oven—and an oven with a stone hearth! American *pizzaiolos* stretch their dough on to pizza screens made of expanded metal—a great idea not yet used in this country. At home I recommend you lower the circle of dough into a round 23-cm (9-inch) pan with sloping edges not more than 3.5 cm (1½ inches) high—which make the pan about 25 cm (10 inches) across at the top. This will give you the traditional shape for your pizza. The 23-cm or 9-inch pan is the one used for the recipes in this book. A pizza of this size will feed one hungry person as a main course, or two people as part of a large meal. You can of course use pans 18 or 20 cm (7 or 8 inches) in diameter if you wish to make smaller pizzas. If you're not particular about the shape, you can just as easily use square or oblong pans.

Mild steel pans are the best, but aluminium or teflon-coated ones are also suitable, and an ordinary sponge cake pan works well. If your tray is new, grease it with pork fat or oil and break it in by putting it in a very hot oven for 10 minutes.

Dough can also be stretched over a flat oven plate to make a bigger pizza and one which is perhaps easier to divide between, say, 6 people as a first course. Be sure to pinch a rim in the dough so that the filling does not spill over in the cooking. This applies to every pizza you make.

Your scales should be accurate. If you have no scales, adopt an alternative measure: a normal tea cup, for instance, holds 224 g (8 oz) liquid and 112 g (4 oz) flour.

As for your oven, you may have no option on that. Let's hope it will reach 260°C (500°F)/Gas 9. Ideally pizzas should be cooked in an oven at 370°C (700°F) and with top and bottom heat. Without this sort of home furnace, you are liable to fall short of perfection, as the dough tends to come out slightly biscuity when baked in a domestic oven. One consolation is that it is easier to eat with your fingers when it is crispy. The variations in results you achieve from one oven to another may be so great that I can only suggest you try it and see. If the preparations are too much and the oven heat too little, you can always pop out to your local pizzeria—if you are lucky enough to have one!

Most domestic ovens will produce good pizzas, but sadly I am reminded of the words of the *padrone* of the Gioia Mia pizzeria in Rome, who said that a wood oven is the *anima della pizza*—its very soul. One of my greatest problems while writing this book has been to find a way of cooking a perfect pizza in a domestic oven. It is almost a contradiction in terms, but I am sure you will have success with one of the following dough recipes.

Dough recipes

There are several recipes you can use to provide the base for the pizza, but the one I call the *basic dough* and generally suggest in the recipes gives the nearest approximation to an authentic Italian pizza. If you find the other doughs work well, by all means use them; but remember that although they may taste good, they may be nothing like the pizza you would eat in either Naples or a pizzeria. I suggest you use 224 grammes (8 ounces) of flour in most of the dough recipes, because that will be sufficient for two standard pizzas. You may not wish to make two at a time, but I recommend you always make up the suggested quantity of basic dough. If you have more than you require, you can freeze the dough after it has been kneaded or you can allow the surplus to rise, roll it out in the usual way and bake it for ten minutes, without topping, in a hot oven. After it has cooked, wrap the base in polythene and put it in the freezer. It will be ready for a quick pizza on another occasion: just add the topping and put it in a hot oven for fifteen minutes—there is no need to let it thaw first.

Basic dough

1.5 dl ($\frac{1}{4}$ pint) water
1 level teaspoon sugar
14 g ($\frac{1}{2}$ oz) fresh yeast or 2 level teaspoons dried yeast
224 g (8 oz) plain flour
1$\frac{1}{2}$ level teaspoons salt
oil

1 Measure the tepid water—about 27°C (80°F)—into a bowl.
2 Add the sugar.
3 Squeeze the fresh yeast in the liquid with your fingers and swirl the liquid until sugar and yeast are dissolved. If using dried yeast, sprinkle it over the surface of the water and whisk it into the liquid with a fork until yeast and sugar are dissolved, and allow the mixture to stand for 10–15 minutes in a warm place until froth develops on the surface.
4 Sift the flour and the salt into a large mixing bowl.
5 Pour in the yeast liquid.
6 Lightly oil or flour your hands.
7 Work the flour and liquid together until it becomes a coherent mass.
8 Sprinkle your work surface generously with flour.
9 Tip dough on to the work surface and scrape out any which is sticking to the bowl.
10 Begin kneading. You may already have an established method of kneading dough, and certainly you will develop your individual technique. If you have never done this before, I suggest you pull the far edge of the dough in towards the centre with one hand and push it down and away from you with the heel of the other hand, developing a rhythmical rolling motion as you do so. The kneading process mixes the flour and liquid and strengthens and develops the gluten which holds the gas bubbles generated by the yeast.
11 Continue kneading for about five minutes, until the doughball

becomes smooth and silky. It should not be sticking to your fingers or to the work surface by this stage.

12 If the dough is still wet and sticky after a few minutes' kneading, flour the work surface again so that more flour is worked into the doughball. If the dough is too stiff and dry, add a little tepid water, no more than half a teaspoonful at a time. The humidity in the atmosphere, and the type of flour you are using, can make these adjustments necessary. True *pizzaiolos* can sniff the air on waking up and know by instinct just how much water to put in the dough. It is sometimes quite tricky to get the consistency right, but practice makes perfect.

13 When the dough has become a soft and supple ball, rinse the mixing bowl with cold water to remove any last remnants of flour, dry it, sprinkle in a touch of flour or rub a couple of drops of olive oil over the surface, and place the doughball in it. Cover with a damp cloth and allow to stand somewhere warm for approximately one hour. Place the bowl clear of draughts but not in direct heat. An airing cupboard works well but, more often than not, it is just as satisfactory to leave the bowl on your work surface.

If you do not wish to make the pizzas for several hours, the dough can be placed at the bottom of your refrigerator. Yeast does not work at temperatures below 4.5°C (40°F), but providing your refrigerator is not that cold the dough will start to rise very slowly. When you take it out of the fridge, put it in a warm place and leave it until it is approximately twice its original size. If you are short of time, the dough will rise faster if you use slightly warmer water—about 38°C (100°F). *Hot* water must *not* be used. It is frequently recommended that the dough be placed in an oiled polythene bag, sufficiently large to allow it to expand. Try it if you like, but I find it more trouble that way.

14 Contain your impatience for at least three-quarters of an hour by relaxing with a drink. You can be gently preparing your ingredients and pizza trays ready for the filling at this stage. You even have time to go out and buy them from the local shop if necessary!

15 After about an hour the dough should have expanded considerably, and be roughly twice its original size. Rub a little oil or flour on your fingers and reach down underneath the dough by running your fingers down the side of the bowl. Gently lift the dough up and punch it down again. This is known by bakers as 'knocking back' the dough and releases large air bubbles which might make the pizza uneven.

---

1 Forming the dough into a coherent mass   2 Kneading   3 The doughball after proving   4 Knocking back   5 If you must use a rolling pin, use one hand only and exert very little pressure   6 Add tomato, mozzarella, and other ingredients as desired

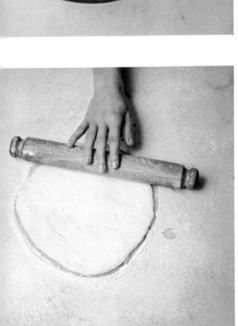

16 Divide the dough into two equal sections by pinching it in the middle with your thumb and forefinger. You should now have two lumps of dough each weighing approximately 196 g (7 oz). Roll each piece into a ball on the palm of your hand, until it is sealed underneath. If you cannot seal it, nip the cracks together, and place the two balls on the lightly-floured work surface. Cover them with an upturned mixing bowl, a damp cloth, or silver foil and allow them to rest for 10–20 minutes.

17 Preheat the oven to 230–260°C (450–500°F)/Gas 8–9. Discovering the temperature at which your oven best cooks pizzas might be a matter of trial and error; if your oven tends to be a hot one, I would suggest you first try it at 230°C (450°F)/Gas 8. Never put the pizza in the oven until it has reached its full heat.

18 When the doughballs have rested for the additional 10–20 minutes and are soft to the touch but not too springy, they are ready to be stretched and spread into the prepared trays.

Alternative doughs

The dough I have just described produces the nearest thing to an authentic pizzeria pizza base possible when using a domestic cooker. The pizza you make will be substantial enough for a main course—and should be delicious!

In Italy, however, pizzas are often prepared in private homes as the first course for a dinner. A lighter dough is used as the base, which is more appropriate when further dishes are to follow. *Pizza casalinga,* as the domestic variety is called, can be made with one of the following bases. The quantities suggested will make two 23-cm (9-in) pizzas or several smaller ones.

Pasta all'uovo per pizze (Enriched pizza dough)

14 g (½ oz) fresh yeast or 2 level teaspoons dried yeast
4 tablespoons milk
1 teaspoon sugar
224 g (8 oz) plain flour
1½ teaspoons salt
1 egg
28 g (1 oz) butter

Dissolve the yeast in 4 tablespoons of tepid milk. Dissolve the sugar in the liquid. Sift flour and salt together. Add the dissolved yeast mixture and begin to mix to a dough. Add more milk, half a teaspoon at a time, if necessary. Beat the egg and add it to the mixture. Smear the soft butter on the dough, place on a lightly-floured work surface and knead until all the butter is worked into the dough. Place in bowl, cover with a damp cloth and allow to rise for an hour in a warm spot. This dough makes a soft, light crust.

Pizza dough with potato

14 g (½ oz) fresh yeast or 2
  level teaspoons dried yeast
1 teaspoon sugar
1.2 dl (4 oz) water
224 g (8 oz) plain flour
1½ teaspoons salt
70 g (2½ oz) mashed potato,
  unseasoned

I always make this, and many other doughs, directly on the work surface without using a mixing bowl. Add the yeast and sugar to the tepid water and mix until they are thoroughly dissolved. Sift the flour and salt, make a well in the middle and add the potatoes, thoroughly mashed but unseasoned. Add the yeast liquid and mix together. Slowly add a little more water and begin to knead. When you have a soft and supple doughball, put it in a bowl, cover with a damp cloth and leave to rise for at least an hour in a warm place.

Whole wheat dough I

Whole wheat dough tends to make a heavier pizza and one 23-cm (9-in) pizza may be sufficient for 2 people. The lighter dough (II) is generally to be recommended, because it is not so heavy and yet provides a whole wheat flavour. When making these doughs, you may find it improves them to increase slightly the quantity of yeast. It will be easier to spread the whole wheat dough (particularly I) with a rolling pin.

1 teaspoon sugar
1.5 dl (¼ pint) milk and
  water equally mixed
14 g (½ oz) fresh yeast or 2
  level teaspoons dried yeast
224 g (8 oz) 100% whole
  wheat flour, unsifted
1½ level teaspoons salt
14 g (½ oz) butter

Weigh out the ingredients. Dissolve the sugar in the milk and water mixture. Add the yeast and when dissolved mix into the flour and salt. When the water has been absorbed tip the mixture on to a lightly-floured work surface. Rub in the softened butter and knead until the dough becomes smooth. Cover and allow to rest in a warm spot for 1½ to 2 hours. Then divide the dough into 2 equal pieces, cover and allow to rest for 20 minutes.

Whole wheat dough II

1 teaspoon sugar
1.5 dl (¼ pint) milk and
  water equally mixed
14 g (½ oz) fresh yeast or 2
  level teaspoons dried yeast
224 g (8 oz) whole wheat
  flour and plain flour equally
  mixed
1½ level teaspoons salt
14 g (½ oz) butter

Mix to a smooth dough as in recipe I, above.

For a quick pizza dough, which does not require yeast and therefore does not need to be left to prove, I suggest you try the following recipes. Each of them makes enough dough for *one* standard pizza.

Pizza scone dough

112 g (4 oz) self-raising flour
½ teaspoon salt
28 g (1 oz) butter
1 egg, beaten
4 tablespoons milk

Sift flour and salt. Rub in the butter until the mixture looks like sand. Add the beaten egg and milk and mix well with a fork until you have a smooth batter.

Pizzetine dough

112 g (4 oz) self-raising flour
½ teaspoon salt
28 g (1 oz) margarine
2 tablespoons milk

Sift flour and salt. Rub in margarine, adding milk and mixing to a dough. Knead well until a smooth consistency is reached, adding half a teaspoon of milk at a time as necessary.

Frizza dough

112 g (4 oz) plain flour
1 level teaspoon baking
*   powder*
1 level teaspoon salt
4 tablespoons water

Sift flour, baking powder and salt together in a bowl. Add water and mix until you have a stiff dough, adding half a teaspoon of water at a time as necessary to make a coherent mass. Knead until the dough is smooth.

Instant alternatives

Bread mixes, either white or brown, can be used for a pizza base. You can also use frozen croissants: unroll them and lay them side by side, with the perforated edges overlapping, on a large oven tray. A third alternative is frozen puff pastry, which makes a delightful pizza base. If you are very pushed for time but want the idea of a pizza, you can use baps or even slices of bread for the base—but please don't quote me on it (unless you make a Pizza di Scamorza, page 68).

Rolling the dough

Rolling out the dough is an art in itself. The Neapolitans do it marvellously by hand. Starting with plenty of flour on the table they give the doughball a sharp slap, then put one stretched palm flat in the middle of the dough. With this hand they turn the dough while pulling the edge outwards with the other hand, grasping it very lightly as if they were feeling the texture of a fine piece of cloth. Turning and pulling in this way they eventually make a large, thin dough circle which they send spinning in the air above their heads. If this is beyond you then roll it out as they do in Rome and most other places, but please, don't press too hard!

A true *pizzaiolo* never uses a rolling pin. If he is on the lazy side he still will not use a commercial rolling pin, but will saw the end off a broom handle and use that. He uses one hand only, exerting a light pressure on the middle of the baton as he rolls it. Too heavy a rolling can kill the dough and make it very tough.

Prepare your pizza pan by greasing it lightly. Lard is suitable, but a groundnut oil is better. Olive oil tends to smoke. Never use a cheap, anonymous 'cooking oil' or rancid frying oil—for this or for anything else to do with making pizzas.

When you have rolled your dough, put the circle in the pan; pat it gently so that it fits and make the edge of the dough rise a little by tapping it lightly about half an inch from the edge. The dough will expand again in the cooking; not much, but enough to produce a hefty crust if you aren't careful to make sure the uncooked dough is flattened thinly and evenly.

Now your base is complete and you can add the tomato and your chosen filling at once. The finished pizza will take between 15 and 20 minutes to bake, according to your oven.

The collection of recipes in this book includes most classic pizzas and a few originals. As you will see, there are many delicious combinations of ingredients. Common to the majority of them are the basic layer of tomato, the herbs and the topping of cheese.

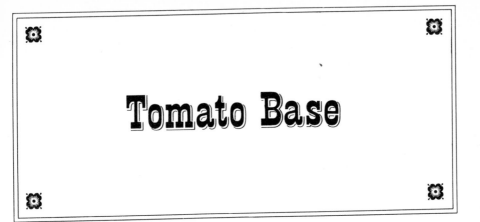

Tomato Base

FOR THE BASIC layer of tomato you may use canned Italian plum tomatoes, fresh ones, or a specially created tomato sauce. I find that 84 grammes (3 ounces) of tomato are adequate for one 23-cm (9-in) pizza.

Canned tomatoes

Put the tomatoes into a basin, season with salt and pepper, and squash them with your fingers. If the tomatoes are not Italian and therefore not sweet you may want to add a little sugar. Try to avoid tomatoes which are canned in water rather than sauce. If you do use them it is best to drain off the water before crushing them. Further aromatics—garlic, crushed bay leaf, fresh chopped basil or oregano—may be added, but they are not really necessary.

Fresh tomatoes

If you are using fresh tomatoes they should be skinned and cored. Skin tomatoes by nicking their skins and pouring boiling water over them. Leave for 30 seconds and you'll find the skins slide off easily. Cut away the hard cores, squash the flesh with your hands and add seasonings to your taste.

Whether the tomatoes are fresh or canned, with or without their own sauce, be sure to taste them for proper seasoning before you put them on the pizza. One of the greatest faults in a pizza is to have the tomato too bland.

Tomato sauce

This makes a much more substantial base for a pizza filling and with a topping of cheese and olives it makes a fine pizza. The recipe will make enough sauce for 4 pizzas.

1 large onion
1 clove garlic
oil
448-g (1-lb) can Italian
    plum tomatoes
2 tablespoons tomato paste
salt and pepper
bay leaf, crushed
oregano

Finely chop the onion and garlic. Cook for about 10 minutes in the oil—just let the vegetables soften, not brown or fry. Add the can of tomatoes, the paste, some salt, a generous screw of black pepper, a bay leaf and a sprinkling of oregano. Stir well, to dissolve and disperse the paste, and leave to simmer and reduce until you have a thickish sauce.

To add variety to the sauce you can add any of the following, all finely chopped, to the onion and garlic: celery, peppers (green or red), leeks, parsley, Italian fennel, carrots.

The sauce keeps well in a screw-top jar in the refrigerator and has many other uses: it goes well with spaghetti and lasagne, with steak and in moussaka, and it makes a nice base for poached eggs or a filling for an omelette.

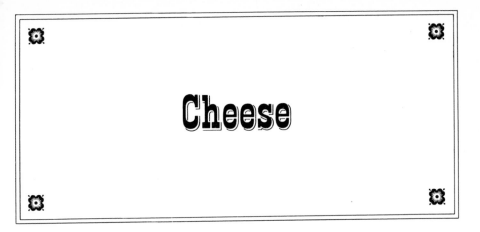

Cheese

THE AUTHENTIC CHESSE of the pizza is *mozzarella*. At one time it was made only from buffalo milk—and it still is in parts of southern Italy. When I expressed doubt about this in the town of Battipaglia, they assured me that it was true but still had to drive me ten miles across country before we finally saw a herd of buffalo sheltering in the shade of a tree.

Mozzarella is a soft, white, mild and delicate cheese. It is usually sold in small quantities, wrapped to preserve the whey that drips from it; this is a sign of freshness. When absolutely new it is a delicious cheese, tender and sweet. Very good mozzarella, or *fior di latte* as it is called when it is not made of buffalo milk, is produced by two Italian firms in this country, Carnevale and Olympia. Italians tell me that the mozzarella available here is actually better than that you will find in Italy because our grass is greener. Recently a dairy in Edinburgh has started to produce Scottish mozzarella with the pizza industry in mind. It is not usually served as a table cheese, but can be quite tasty beneath lots of freshly ground pepper. This cheese cooks extraordinarily well, becoming soft and stringy like no other cheese does. To use mozzarella on a pizza, you can cut it into cubes, slice it, grate it or mince it. It will melt satisfactorily in any of these forms.

Mozzarella is not at present universally available, and it tends to be expensive, but I do urge you to try it on your pizza. As a substitute, the creamy fat cheeses such as Bel Paese, Port Salut, Gouda or Bonbel make adequate alternatives. English cheeses should be used with caution, mainly because their flavour is so familiar from our range of Welsh Rarebits and toasted cheese dishes. That curious melted cheese taste does not blend well with the olives, anchovies and other aromatic ingredients of a pizza. Lancashire cheese cooks well, however, and very often ordinary English Cheddar is a good choice. Experiment to suit your taste.

Other Italian cheeses which can be used for pizza include pecorino and Parmesan (both hard cheeses which must be grated), and ricotta.

Ricotta, which does not melt when cooked, is a form of cream cheese; cottage cheese may be substituted.

As you would expect, the high heat needed to cook pizza means that the cheese will sometimes melt and burn before the dough has cooked. For this reason it is often better to add the cheese at what the Italians call the *mezzo cottura* (halfway) stage. Like other aspects of pizza-making, you will only learn which is best in your oven by experimenting. Foibles of domestic ovens are many, as are variations in cheese. If you can get away with putting on your cheese at the beginning, good luck to you. It is better that way. But if you are going to end up with something that looks like ginger snap, then I would rather you added the cheese at *mezzo cottura*.

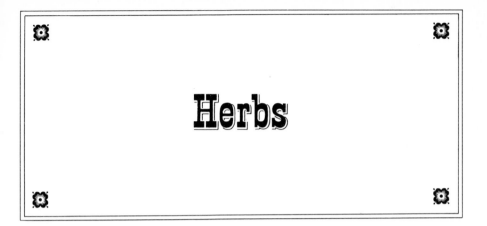

Herbs

Oregano

This herb takes its name from the Greek words meaning 'joy of the mountains' and is the characteristic flavouring of the pizza. A scattering of oregano is as essential as the final sprinkle of salt, pepper and oil. The herb is sometimes confused with marjoram, to which family it belongs. It does not feature much in English cooking, though as marjoram it grows wild on the South Downs. But in any case Italian or Greek oregano has a much stronger scent which is released in cooking and smells delicious.

Basil

Originally from India, basil is now prominent in Italian cooking. Basil is a basic component of the Margherita pizza. It goes exquisitely with tomatoes, but in England seems to be associated only with turtle soup! Basil can be grown easily in pots on a window ledge or in a greenhouse. It produces a lovely bushy plant and its leaves have a sharp, aromatic scent. Failing fresh basil, the dried variety may be used.

Bay leaves

Part of the laurel family, bay leaves were once used to make wreaths to crown heroes of ancient Greece and Rome. A leaf or two crumbled into the basic tomato sauce adds a very pleasant flavour. They should be minced and crumbled finely in order to extract the most flavour.

Garlic

Not a herb, in my opinion, but another essential ingredient in a pizza. One clove, which is a segment of a whole bulb, is enough to flavour one pizza. Take off the papery skin and chop the clove as finely as possible, sprinkling it over the pizza as you go. You may incorporate the flavour into the tomato sauce by cooking a clove or two with the onions. The

37

English are curiously nervous of garlic, so make sure no unsuspecting person finds a large chunk in his mouth. Fresh garlic is best, but dried minced garlic or garlic powder make an adequate substitute. If you are worried about the strong smell of garlic, eat some fresh parsley after your pizza. It is an effective antidote.

Parsley

Italian parsley has flat leaves unlike our own curly variety. I find it easier to cook with though not so decorative. Garnish your pizza with fresh chopped parsley, or add it to the tomato sauce.

Experiment with other herbs in your pizzas. Try thyme, rosemary (with care), chervil and sage (with even more care).

Other Ingredients

Anchovies

Tinned anchovy fillets are easily available. Some are sold rolled up around capers or olives; these are more expensive and their decorative nature may get lost on top of a pizza bursting with cheese. If you find the anchovy fillets too salty, soak them in a little milk before using them. If they seem too big, slit them in half lengthwise—but be sure to do so *before* you soak them. In Soho, most delicatessens sell *alici sotto sale*, which are whole anchovies in salt. These are splendid on pizza, but remember to slit them open and take out the bones before you use them.

Olives

Essential to most pizzas. Try to buy them loose from the delicatessen or grocer; they will be sweeter and juicier and less expensive than those small jars of olives in brine designed for cocktail parties. Stone them or not, as you please—though if you have large black olives they should be halved and stoned before using. Green olives go well with pizza, as do stuffed olives if you feel extravagant.

Oil

A pizza is one of those dishes in which every ingredient adds its own quality to the finished whole. It would be a pity to ruin a carefully prepared dish by using inferior oil. In pizza-making, the oil appears several times: it may be used in making the dough; it is used to grease the pizza pan; and finally used to lubricate the finished article. Use the best oil you can find—olive oil becomes increasingly expensive, but is the best. The imported Italian and Greek oils will most closely resemble the thick, virgin local olive oil used in Italian pizzerias. Of the others, I find groundnut oil the most acceptable. It is heavy and rich and does not smoke so readily.

Capers

A sharp addition to any pizza, capers go particularly well with fish such as tuna. They can only be bought pickled; be sure to buy them pickled in brine and not acid vinegar or they will spoil the pizza. Drain them before use. The best capers come from Morocco, France, Spain and Italy. They are graded in six sizes: non pareils (smallest), surfines, capucines, capôtes, fines and gruesas. The recipes in this book use surfines and capucines.

Pine kernels

An expensive and luxurious addition. They come from the cones of the stone pine and are small, cream-coloured and oily. They are used in Italy in all kinds of cooking, from meat dishes to cakes. You can usually buy them at health food shops—but at a high price considering they are frequently put out like peanuts in Mediterranean bars.

Green hot peppers

Sometimes called pepperoni, or pepperoncini, these are available fresh, canned or bottled. They are very sharp but will please many a pizza connoisseur. Use them whole or chopped into several pieces.

Green peppers

These are capsicums, the fresh variety of peppers available at most greengrocers, and should not be confused with green hot peppers. Discard the seeds and chop the casing into small pieces—a wonderfully colourful garnish to a pizza.

Zanzibar chillies

Small red peppers, varying in size from 1 to 5 cm ($\frac{1}{2}$ to 2 in). They are very hot and many people like them crushed on their pizza. Let your guests do this themselves and don't touch delicate parts of your body after crumbling them, or you will feel as if you are in a bed of nettles.

Red and yellow peppers

These are mild in flavour. Chopped up they are known as pepperonata.

A Word of Advice

AS YOU WILL see from the following recipes there is very little in the way of meat, fish, vegetables and fruit that cannot go on top of a pizza. Few dishes lend themselves to such imaginative treatment.

This does not mean, however, that the pizza can be regarded as the rag-bag of the kitchen. A handful of various left-overs taken from the fridge and spread on a dough base will not necessarily make a good pizza. Simplicity and balance are the keynotes; restrict the amount of ingredients used on each pizza and make sure the things you do use blend or contrast nicely.

Do not overfill a pizza. I have sometimes been carried away when topping an uncooked pizza in one of my experimental sessions—it begins to look amazingly attractive, another olive here, a little more cheese there, and so on. Remember that the dough will expand a little when it starts to cook, cheese melts and bubbles and before you know where you are, the whole thing has overflowed in the oven and is difficult, if not impossible, to eat. When it goes into your oven, a pizza should look underfilled rather than overfilled.

Pizza is substantial food. The dough base is filling enough, so when topping it, avoid any further heavy ingredient which would overdo the starch content; you *can* use flour-based sauces, potatoes, or even beans on pizza—but it does unbalance the dish. That said, those of you who, like myself, seem to thrive on starch, will find some recipes in the following pages which, though adding starch to starch, are still delicious.

Some final reminders

*When washing your hands, utensils or work surfaces after making the dough, always use cold water, as this removes the flour more easily.

*Doughballs wrapped in clear film will stay usable for a couple of days or so if left at the bottom of your fridge. They must be given plenty of time to develop in a warmer atmosphere before you use them.

*If accidentally you leave the doughball uncovered for too long and it develops a crust, cover with a damp cloth and the skin will disappear.

*In most domestic ovens, the hottest and best place to cook a pizza is right at the top. Experiment until you find the hottest spot in your oven.

*Flour and water are the original glue. Don't expect your kitchen to be in good shape after cooking a pizza.

*Aim to cook the dough to a 't'. The edge must not be too high, but high enough to stop the ingredients running out. When you pinch the edge after cooking, it should snap slightly. If in doubt, overcook rather than undercook. Should the pizza seem too dry, add more oil when it comes out of the oven.

*Don't worry that your dough will be too thick. Thickness will not kill a pizza as long as the dough is light and airy.

*Different pans will give different results. Whenever possible, test them before cooking for an important occasion.

*If you have a chance to cook your pizza in an oven with a stone floor, take it. Dispense with the metal pans. It will need skilful handling to slide the pizza on to the hearth, Neapolitan style, and you will really require a proper wooden peel to slide it into the oven and a metal one to take it out. Be sure to yell out the old *pizzaiolos'* vibrant cry when the pizzas go in or out of the oven—'*Pronto c'a pala*', or 'Ready with the peel'.

*Don't meddle with the doughball once you have rounded it and sealed it. The doughball will take care of itself!

*A *pizzaiolo* makes a *pizzico* or pinch of an ingredient with three fingers, not five.

*On cool nights you can allow the dough to rise overnight. You can also use your refrigerator, but be sure to keep the doughball well away from the freezing compartment (yeast does not grow at temperatures below 4.5°C (40°F)). If you leave the dough to rise overnight in the fridge, allow it to return to room temperature before stretching it out.

*Always use the best quality ingredients. Then whatever happens in the cooking, at least your results will be edible.

*Wine goes very well with pizza. Dough-making is quite a long and warm process, so remember to bring home an extra bottle of vino to keep you and any observers going during the preparation!

*Inventiveness can reach its peak when cooking pizzas. There is almost nothing you cannot top them with, and the bases are legion too. So let your fancy have full rein when you are your own *pizzaiolo*, from the simplest and most classic combinations to the most unusual. Keep experimenting!

The Pizzas of PizzaExpress

Note: All the recipes in this book make one 23-cm (9-in) pizza, unless otherwise stated. For notes on the preparation and use of standard pizza ingredients, and their substitutes, please read pages 21–42 above.

Margherita

The story of the Margherita has been told earlier. It is my favourite pizza and is really the foundation for almost every pizza you will ever wish to make.

196 g (7 oz) basic dough
84 g (3 oz) tomato
olive oil
56 g (2 oz) mozzarella
salt and pepper
2 or 3 basil leaves

Spread the dough in a lightly-greased pan. Cover with tomato almost to the edge. Sprinkle with oil and distribute the mozzarella over the tomato. Add salt, pepper and basil leaves. Place in a hot oven, 230°C (450°F)/Gas 8, for 20 minutes or until the dough has cooked through.

Variations

Oregano can be substituted for basil.

To vary the taste and texture of the cheese, add a *pizzico* of Parmesan to the mozzarella, or cut more mozzarella into thin slices and spread them over the surface 5 minutes before the pizza is cooked.

A sprinkling of red chilli peppers goes well on a Margherita for those who like their pizzas hot.

An unusual American variation which tastes good is used by Larry Goldberg: he puts the tomato over the cheese, so that it is covered completely, advising that you press the tomato well into the cheese. Different, but try it sometime!

A Margherita Bianca is a classic Italian pizza, made in the same way as the Margherita, but without tomato. Add plenty of coarse salt and oil. For an even simpler Pizza Bianca, cook the dough and just add oil, coarse salt, pepper and rosemary or basil.

43

Napoletana I

196 g (7 oz) basic dough	Line a lightly-greased pan with the dough.
84 g (3 oz) tomato	Spread the tomato almost to the edge and
56 g (2 oz) mozzarella	distribute the cheese evenly over the pizza.
1 anchovy	Break the anchovy into two or three pieces and
10 capers	put these on the cheese, with the capers and
3 olives	olives. Season with salt and pepper, add some
salt and pepper	oregano and sprinkle with oil. Place in the hot
oregano	oven, 230°C (450°F)/Gas 8, for 20 minutes or
oil	until the dough is cooked.

Variations

For a true Napoletana you only need the tomato and anchovy; capers and olives may be omitted.

To make the pizza more decorative, you can use more anchovy pieces and arrange them in a lattice on the top. Don't worry if the anchovy seems to disappear in cooking—it's still there and you will certainly taste it.

Napoletana II

Thought by the Romans to be the true pizza, this is called Pizza Romana by the Neapolitans!

196 g (7 oz) basic dough	Spread the dough in a lightly-greased pan and
84 g (3 oz) tomato	cover with tomato almost to the edge. Arrange
6 anchovies	the other ingredients on top and cook for 20
salt and pepper	minutes at 230°C (450°F)/Gas 8.
basil leaf	
56 g (2 oz) mozzarella	
14 g ($\frac{1}{2}$ oz) Parmesan	
oil	

Mushroom

196 g (7 oz) basic dough	Line a lightly-greased pan with the dough and
84 g (3 oz) tomato	top with tomato almost to the edge. Thinly
56 g (2 oz) button mushrooms	slice the mushrooms—it's best to use fresh
42 g (1$\frac{1}{2}$ oz) mozzarella	ones, but tinned ones will do—and arrange
garlic	them on the tomato. (If you feel it is necessary
pepper and salt	to wash the mushrooms, be sure to dry them
oregano	well, or they will give the pizza a soupy
oil	consistency.)

Sprinkle the cheese over the pizza. Add a few pieces of very finely chopped or crushed garlic, plenty of pepper, a pinch of salt and some oregano. Lightly sprinkle with oil and place in a hot oven, 230°C (450°F)/Gas 8, for 20 minutes.

Maschera Napoletana

" *Vi che pizza nu turnese,
magnatélla a stu paese.* "

Variations

Chopped parsley may be sprinkled over the mushrooms and grated Parmesan makes a good alternative to mozzarella.

Champignons de Paris, cut lengthwise, look very pleasing on a mushroom pizza.

Neptune

For many years we included cheese on this pizza. Add it if you wish, but I think that it tastes better without.

196 g (7 oz) basic dough	Spread the dough in a lightly-greased pan.
84 g (3 oz) tomato	Cover with tomato almost to the edge. Break
56 g (2 oz) tuna	up the tuna into small chunks and spread over
4 thin slices of onion	the tomato. Decorate with rings of onion (be
10 capers	sure to slice them *very* thinly), the capers and
3 olives	the olives. Break up the anchovies into two or
2 anchovies	three pieces and put these on the pizza. Add
salt and pepper	salt—but not too much as the anchovy is very
oil	salty—and pepper and sprinkle with oil. Cook in a hot oven, 230°C (450°F)/Gas 8, for 20 minutes.

Veneziana (Pizza in Saor)

This pizza resulted from an idea we had to help stop Venice from falling into the lagoon. We decided to offer a Pizza Veneziana and add a surcharge for the Venice in Peril Fund.

I made my enquiries in Venice to find out what the locals considered to be a Venetian pizza but rather drew a blank as pizza is not indigenous to this area of Italy. I received suggestions to include everything from bacallà (dried cod) to a certain type of Venetian bean, from scampi to black ink fish.

This particular recipe was given to me by Signor Rusconi of the Gritti Palace Hotel in Venice, who kindly obtained it from Signor Massimo Alberini, a famous Italian gourmet and cookery writer. He called it Pizza in Saor, inspired by a famous sole dish of that name. Saor (Venetian for '*sapore*' meaning savour) is a marinade made from onions, white wine, vinegar, sugar, raisins and pine kernels. 'Sfogie in saor', the sole dish, dates from the Middle Ages.

196 g (7 oz) basic dough	Spread the dough in a lightly-greased pan.
14 g (½ oz) pine kernels	Cover with pine kernels and sultanas, then add
28 g (1 oz) sultanas	the tomato sauce. Cover with the thinly-sliced
56 g (2 oz) tomato	onion rings, olives and capers. Sprinkle with

---

Pulcinello, a folkloric Neapolitan character symbolising the poor people of his city who undertake all common tasks in order to earn a living. Here he is seen singing the praises of his local pizzeria

28 g (1 oz) onions, thinly
 sliced
5 black olives, pitted
10 capers, in brine
oil
14 g (½ oz) mozzarella
oregano
salt and pepper

oil, add a very light sprinkling of mozzarella and oregano. Season with salt and pepper and cook in a hot oven, 230°C (450°F)/Gas 8, for 20 minutes.

Onion and Anchovy

196 g (7 oz) basic dough
84 g (3 oz) tomato
1 onion, thinly sliced
4 anchovies
42 g (1½ oz) mozzarella
salt and pepper
oregano
oil

Spread the dough evenly in a lightly-greased pan and top with tomato almost to the edge. Add the onion rings, and the anchovies broken into two or three pieces. Sprinkle the mozzarella over the pizza and season with salt, pepper and oregano. Add a little oil and cook for 20 minutes in a hot oven, 230°C (450°F)/Gas 8.

Variations

You can substitute 2 teaspoons of grated Parmesan for the mozzarella, or use both cheeses together.

Mix in shallots, thinly sliced, or a spring onion or two for variety.

Pietro

Many *pizzaiolos* have been called 'Pizza Pete' since the time when Don Pietro ran the Pizzeria Brandi in Naples in the 1870s. This pizza, with its pleasant flavour, was christened in honour of all Pizza Petes, wherever they may be.

196 g (7 oz) basic dough *84 g (3 oz) tomato* *42 g (1½ oz) mozzarella* *4 anchovies* *3 olives* *salt and pepper* *oregano* *oil*	Spread the dough in a lightly-greased pan. Cover with tomato almost to the edge. Add the cheese, sprinkling it evenly over the pizza. Arrange the anchovies, either by breaking them up or by placing them spoke fashion around the pizza, splitting them down the middle if they are too large. Add the olives. Season, sprinkle with oil and bake in a hot oven, 230°C (450°F)/Gas 8, for 20 minutes.

Marinara

This pizza is often known as Pizza Napoletana in Naples, and is perhaps the oldest pizza. It has no cheese but has a clean flavour, provided you like anchovies.

196 g (7 oz) basic dough *84 g (3 oz) tomato* *4 anchovies* *1 garlic clove* *6 olives* *oil* *salt and pepper*	Line a lightly-greased pan with the dough. Spread the tomato almost to the edge. Break each anchovy into two or three pieces and arrange on the tomato. Add the garlic, finely chopped, and the olives. Sprinkle with oil, add salt and pepper and cook in a hot oven, 230°C (450°F)/Gas 8, for 20 minutes.

Four Seasons

This is our most popular pizza. It's a delicious combination, but do be careful not to overload it.

196 g (7 oz) basic dough *84 g (3 oz) tomato* *42 g (1½ oz) mozzarella* *28 g (1 oz) mushrooms* *28 g (1 oz) pepperoni sausage* *2 anchovies* *3 olives* *10 capers* *salt and pepper* *oregano* *oil*	Spread the dough in a lightly-greased pan and top with tomato almost to the edge. Put the mozzarella on one quarter of the pizza, the sliced mushrooms on another, the pepperoni on a third quarter and the anchovies on the fourth. Dot the pizza with the olives and capers. Add salt, pepper, oregano and a little oil to each section, remembering not to put much oil on the pepperoni section or too much salt on the anchovy section. Cook in a hot oven, 230°C (450°F)/Gas 8, for 20 minutes.

Note: You can divide the pizza into four sections by reserving a little of the dough, rolling it out into two thin strips and placing the strips on the tomato sauce to make a cross. If you use three thin strips of pastry, you will, of course, have six sections, and can add two other ingredients of your choice. And why not have six seasons after all!

Four Seasons, Neapolitan Style

Thoroughly wash some cockles and mussels (about a handful) and cook them in boiling water until the shells open. Take out the molluscs. Make a cross on the pizza and fill one quarter with cockles, another with black pitted olives and pieces of anchovy, the third with artichokes in oil and the fourth with mussels. (If you prefer, you may add the cooked mussels at the halfway stage.) Sprinkle with oil and season well. To create a stronger flavour, use raw mussels. To remove the molluscs, open the shells with a knife, and be sure to remove the beard.

Another traditional combination is with sliced pitted green olives, artichoke hearts, mozzarella and anchovies.

Capricciosa

This pizza, as its name implies, is a lighthearted affair on which you can put almost anything you wish. Italian *pizzaiolos* often do!

196 g (7 oz) basic dough
84 g (3 oz) tomato
14 g ($\frac{1}{2}$ oz) ham
1 anchovy
10 capers
3 olives
42 g (1$\frac{1}{2}$ oz) mozzarella
salt and pepper
oregano
oil
1 egg, hard-boiled

Spread the dough in a lightly-greased pan. Spread the tomato almost to the edge. Cut the ham into bite-sized pieces and arrange on the pizza. Add the anchovy, split into two or three pieces, and the capers, olives and cheese. Season with salt, pepper and oregano, sprinkle with a liberal amount of oil and bake in a hot oven, 230°C (450°F)/Gas 8, for 20 minutes. Chop the hard-boiled egg, mix in some salt and add to the pizza before serving.

Variation

Instead of using a hard-boiled egg, you can crack a raw egg on to the part-cooked pizza at the halfway stage and let it cook with the rest of the ingredients.

La Reine (Francescana)

196 g (7 oz) basic dough
84 g (3 oz) tomato
28 g (1 oz) mushrooms
28 g (1 oz) ham
42 g (1$\frac{1}{2}$ oz) mozzarella
garlic
3 olives
salt and pepper
oregano
oil

Spread the dough in a lightly-greased pan. Cover with tomato almost to the edge. Add the mushrooms, sliced. Cut the ham into small pieces and place over the mushrooms. Distribute the cheese evenly over the pizza. Add a soupçon of garlic and the olives. Season with salt, pepper and oregano, sprinkle with oil and bake in a hot oven, 230°C (450°F)/Gas 8, for 20 minutes.

American

Purists do not recognise the existence of salami sausage on a pizza. One of my first American customers, way back in 1965, gave such a glowing description of how his favourite pizza parlour in Florida covered the pizza with wafer-thin slices of salami, that I felt I had to introduce this variety and call it an 'American'.

196 g (7 oz) basic dough
84 g (3 oz) tomato
42 g (1½ oz) thinly-sliced
  pepperoni sausage
42 g (1½ oz) cheese, diced
salt and pepper
oregano

Line a lightly-greased pan with the dough. Spread the tomato almost to the edge. Add the pepperoni slices—about 12—and then cover the pizza with cheese. Add a little salt and pepper and a sprinkling of oregano. No oil is required on the American; enough is produced by the sausage. Cook in a hot oven, 230°C (450°F)/Gas 8, for 20 minutes.

Hungarian gyula is the best pepperoni sausage, but it cannot always be obtained. Hungarian czabas is the next best; you can also use German kabana, Spanish chorizos or any good quality salami. None of these, though, is as good as the gyula sausage.

The Danes are trying hard to beat the Hungarians at their own game and an excellent Danish pepperoni is coming on the market. Late in the field, but equally good, is an English pepperoni. In the United States they are marketing a pepperoni sausage made from spun vegetable protein, which the makers claim will not shrink or curl on the pizza. Whatever the sausage, it must be sliced as thinly as possible; too much of it will make the pizza greasy and heavy.

American Hot

Many is the time I've stood in Andy (son of Harry) McElhone's American bar in Paris (just tell the taxi driver 'Sank Roo Donoo'!), looking at his old machine for keeping sausages hot. The sausages were known as 'Red Hots' and it seemed natural to call our peppery pizza an American Hot. It is one of our most popular pizzas. I like to have it spiced even more with Zanzibar chillies.

The American Hot is assembled in the same way as the American, but add 56 g (2 oz) hot tinned peppers, whole or sliced, before cooking. The peppers may be the long thin variety, or the stubbier type. Use fresh green pepper if you wish, but the pizza will not be as tangy—though it may look more colourful. Jalapenos (*very* hot green peppers) also go well on this pizza.

Four Cheeses (Quattro Formaggi)

196 g (7 oz) basic dough
84 g (3 oz) tomato
14 g (½ oz) mozzarella
14 g (½ oz) Bel Paese
14 g (½ oz) Edam or Gouda
14 g (½ oz) Gruyère or
  Emmentaler
salt and pepper
oregano
oil

Spread the dough in a lightly-greased pan and cover with tomato almost to the edge. Sprinkle the diced cheeses over the pizza. Add the salt, pepper and oregano, and sprinkle with oil. Place in a hot oven, 230°C (450°F)/Gas 8, for 20 minutes or until the dough is cooked through.

Variations

Lancashire, Cheddar, ricotta (or cottage cheese), provolone, Parmesan and many other good melting cheeses can be substituted for the four mentioned here.

To add interest, separate the cheeses, putting each of the four in a separate quarter of the pizza. This allows you to add different herbs to different sections, such as chives on the ricotta, rosemary on the Parmesan, and parsley anywhere you like. You can separate the sections by reserving a little of the dough, rolling it into two thin strips, and making them into a cross on the tomato sauce before adding the cheeses.

Prawn

196 g (7 oz) basic dough
84 g (3 oz) tomato
112 g (4 oz) peeled prawns
42 g (1½ oz) mozzarella
olives
salt and pepper
oregano
dash tabasco
oil

Spread the dough in a lightly-greased pan and top with the tomato almost to the edge. Add all the other ingredients. Cook for 20 minutes in a hot oven, 230°C (450°F)/Gas 8.

A Leaning Tower of Pizzas

Pizza Fiorentina

196 g (7 oz) basic dough
84 g (3 oz) tomato
2 or 3 leaves spinach, washed
28 g (1 oz) mozzarella
28 g (1 oz) Parmesan
salt and pepper
oil
garlic
oregano

Spread the dough evenly in a lightly-greased pan. Cover with tomato almost to the edge. Top with leaf spinach, but be careful not to obscure all the tomato. Add the mozzarella. Sprinkle with grated Parmesan and add salt, pepper, oil, garlic and oregano. Cook for 20 minutes at 230°C (450°F)/Gas 8.

Onion and a dash of nutmeg enhance this pizza.

Cockney Pride Pizza—Apples and Pears

196 g (7 oz) basic dough
84 g (3 oz) tomato
42 g (1½ oz) cheese
2–3 slices pear, diced
2–3 slices apple, diced
nutmeg
cinnamon
salt and pepper
oil

Spread the dough in a lightly-greased pan. Cover with tomato sauce almost to the edge, and top with cheese. Dust the fruit with nutmeg and cinnamon and scatter over the pizza. Add salt, pepper and oil. Cook in a hot oven, 230°C (450°F)/Gas 8, for 20 minutes.

Variations

Pecorino cheese is best for this pizza.
    You can also add a few sultanas, small pieces of bacon and onion.
    Mango chutney, too, can be added to taste.

Pizza Giardiniera

196 g (7 oz) basic dough
84 g (3 oz) tomato
oregano

Lightly grease a pan and line with the dough. Cover with tomato almost to the edge. Sprinkle with oregano. Spread a thin layer of

a very small quantity of any
of the following vegetables :
  leaf spinach ; peas ; sweet
  corn ; asparagus tips ;
  chopped celery ; sliced fresh
  tomato ; potato (boiled and
  sliced) ; onion (thinly
  sliced or chopped) ; fresh
  green pepper ; sliced
  radish ; sliced or chopped
  pimento
42 g (1½ oz) mozzarella
1 dessertspoon grated
  Parmesan
1 artichoke heart
1 olive
salt and pepper
oil
chives

the vegetables over the tomato (be careful not to lay them on too thick or the result will be a stodgy mess). Add the mozzarella and sprinkle with Parmesan. Put the artichoke heart in the centre of the pizza, garnished with an olive. Add salt, pepper and oil. Cook in a hot oven, 230°C (450°F)/Gas 8, for 20 minutes. Scatter a few fresh chopped chives over the pizza before serving.

Vegetarian Pizza

This is a pizza recommended by the Vegetarian Society. It uses wholemeal flour and has a different dough formula from those given earlier. Try it with one of the whole wheat dough recipes on page 30, for some variation.

FOR THE DOUGH :
168 g (6 oz) wholemeal flour
¼ teaspoon sea salt
14 g (½ oz) yeast or 1
  teaspoon dried yeast
¼ cup warm milk
1 small beaten egg
1 teaspoon oil
FOR THE TOPPING :
1 large onion, chopped
1 garlic clove, crushed
oil for frying
4 large skinned and sliced
  tomatoes
6 black olives
marjoram or basil
salt and pepper
olive oil
84 g (3 oz) thinly-sliced
  Cheddar cheese

Sift the flour and salt together into a warm bowl. Prepare the yeast with the warm milk. Mix the beaten egg into the flour and add the yeast liquid. Knead to a soft dough, place in a lightly-oiled container and leave to prove in a warm place for 30 minutes. When it has risen, knead the dough again, pat it out flat on an oiled baking sheet, brush with oil and leave to prove for five more minutes. Fry the onion and garlic in oil, drain and use to cover the pizza base. Add the tomatoes, olives, herbs and seasoning, then sprinkle with olive oil and add cheese slices. Bake for about 20 minutes at 220°C (425°F)/Gas 6.

Variations
Instead of cheese, you may add Granose nut meat or Saviand, cut into small lumps and tossed in oil.

Chicago

This is a totally unofficial name for a pizza using ground or minced beef. I had my first American pizza at a pizzeria in Chicago, a city famous for its stockyards. Therefore it seemed fitting that the Windy City should give its name to this combination.

196 g (7 oz) basic dough
84 g (3 oz) tomato
salt and pepper
28 g (1 oz) chopped onion
  (optional)
56 g (2 oz) minced beef
42 g (1½ oz) cheese
  (American processed or
  Gruyère)
oregano
oil

Spread the dough in a lightly-greased pan. Cover with tomato almost to the edge. Add salt and pepper and the chopped onion to the mince, then spread the mixture over the tomato. Add the cheese, more salt and pepper, oregano and oil. Cook for 20 minutes in a hot oven, 230°C (450°F)/Gas 8.

Chinese Pizza

This pizza was developed in honour of the Chinese New Year—a time when our original Soho pizzeria looks more like our Hong Kong branch!

196 g (7 oz) basic dough
84 g (3 oz) tomato
56–84 g (2–3 oz) beanshoots
56 g (2 oz) prawns
56 g (2 oz) mushrooms
1 tablespoon sliced green
  pepper
salt and pepper
sesame oil

Line a lightly-greased pan with the dough. Spread the tomato almost to the edge. Bake for 10 minutes at 230°C (450°F)/Gas 8. Remove the pizza and cover with beanshoots, prawns, sliced mushrooms and green pepper. Add salt, pepper and oil. Return the pizza to the oven and cook for a further 10 minutes.

Variations

You can add sliced water chestnuts to this pizza and a dash of soy sauce will add to the piquancy. Try, too, a light sprinkling of sesame seeds.

Pizza Inglese

196 g (7 oz) basic dough
84 g (3 oz) tomato
42 g (1½ oz) cheese
1–2 rashers bacon, trimmed
1 egg
oil
salt and pepper
Worcestershire sauce

Spread the dough in a lightly-greased pan. Spread the tomato almost to the edge. Cover with diced cheese. Add bite-sized pieces of bacon, leaving a circle of about 7 or 8 cm (3 in) clear in the centre of the pizza. Place the pizza in a hot oven, 230°C (450°F)/Gas 8, and cook for 10–15 minutes. Remove from oven and break the egg on to the middle of the pizza. Sprinkle a little oil, salt and pepper all over, especially on the egg. Add a dash of Worcestershire sauce, return to the oven and cook for 5 more minutes.

Variations

You can also cook the egg separately and add it to the pizza just before serving. If you choose this method you can serve the egg scrambled, poached or soft- or hard-boiled. Be sure, though, that the egg is still hot when you add it to the pizza.

There are many other variations of pizza using eggs. Here is one you might try, known as pizza *con le uova*. Prepare a Margherita (page 43) using half the amount of cheese and one anchovy. At the halfway stage, crack a couple of eggs on the pizza, add the rest of the cheese and a sprinkle of Parmesan, salt and pepper. If you wish, you may beat the eggs before putting them on the pizza.

Calzone

Watch this being made in an Italian pizzeria, such as Ivo's in Trastevere, or by that master of pizzas, Pasqualino in Naples. In Italian, the word *calzone* means trousers. It is the doyen of pizza variants!

196 g (7 oz) basic dough
1 egg
28 g (1 oz) Italian sausage★
28 g (1 oz) salami
28 g (1 oz) mortadella or ham
28 g (1 oz) ricotta
salt and pepper
oil
28 g (1 oz) tomato
28 g (1 oz) mozzarella
oregano

Roll out the dough into a 20-cm (8-in) circle with a depth of about 0.5 cm ($\frac{1}{4}$ in). Beat the egg, add a little salt and brush the edges of the dough disc with some of the egg mixture. Place small pieces of sausage, salami and mortadella on the half of the dough nearest to you. Add the ricotta, salt, pepper and a touch of oil. The ingredients should form a mound about 2 to 5 cm (1 to 2 in) high. Fold the other half of the dough towards you and *'fa imbaciare'*—make the two parts kiss, as the Italians say—to form a half moon. Press the edges together well, so that the ingredients don't burst out when baking. On the lower slopes of the Calzone place some tomato and seasoned mozzarella; brush the rest of the slope with the remaining egg. Make a small hole at the top of the pastry to let the air escape. Place on a baking sheet and cook for 20 minutes in a hot oven, 230°C (450°F)/Gas 8. The Calzone should emerge beautifully tanned, with a smile on the outside and simmering with delights inside. Just cut it open and eat. It is the nearest thing to bliss this side of Vesuvius.

Note: The Calzone is delicious deep-fried in oil. When you fry it, you don't need to add ingredients on the outer edge, or make a hole in the top.

★Italian sausage is the soft variety known as lucanica and looks like an extended version of the English chipolata, though redder in colour. It is now made in England and is available in delicatessens. English pork or beef sausage make an acceptable substitute.

Pizza Olympico

This was invented at a pizzeria in Amalfi in honour of the Olympic Games in Rome in 1960, but its origins probably go back much farther than that. Needless to say, the colours are those of Italy.

196 g (7 oz) basic dough
84 g (3 oz) tomato
2 or 3 spinach leaves
56 g (2 oz) mozzarella
oil
· salt and pepper
oregano
1 egg cup (white porcelain if
  possible)
sambuca (or any other
  inflammable spirit)
2 coffee beans

Spread the dough in a lightly-greased pan and top with tomato almost to the edge. Add the spinach leaves, which may be cooked or not, as you prefer, to the pizza, avoiding the centre area. Cover the spinach with mozzarella. Add oil, salt, pepper and oregano. Cook in a hot oven, 230°C (450°F)/Gas 8, for 20 minutes. When the pizza is ready, remove it from the oven. Fill the egg cup with sambuca and fix it firmly into the centre of the pizza. Add the coffee beans to the spirit, set light to it, and proceed triumphantly to the table.

Pizza Flambée

Napoleon may not have invented the pizza (though a Frenchman once told me he did), but his countrymen have developed pizza *flambée*. A pizza doused with pre-warmed cognac or grappa and set alight has a pleasing and different taste. You can try it on almost any pizza you like; it goes especially well on fruit pizza.

Francoforte

196 g (7 oz) basic dough
84 g (3 oz) tomato
56–84 g (2–3 oz) sauerkraut
1 frankfurter sausage
42 g (1½ oz) cheese
salt and pepper
caraway seeds
oil

Line a lightly-greased pan with the dough. Spread the tomato almost to the edge. Cover lightly with sauerkraut. Cut the frankfurter with a sharp knife into 0.5-cm (¼-in) slices and distribute evenly over the pizza. Add the cheese. Sprinkle with salt and pepper and a few caraway seeds. Place in a hot oven, 230°C (450°F)/Gas 8, for 20 minutes.

The real frankfurters, from Neu Isenberg, just outside Frankfurt, are ideal for this pizza, but you can substitute Vienna sausages.

Mozzarella is very suitable for this pizza, but Emmentaler or Tilsit also go very well with it.

Thinly sliced shallots can be added.

Sloppy Guiseppe Pizza

This is based on a well-known American dish called Sloppy Joe, which is a type of Mexican barbecue hamburger sauce.

196 g (7 oz) basic dough
56 g (2 oz) minced beef
1 tablespoon finely-chopped green pepper
1 tablespoon finely-chopped onion
3 teaspoons tomato purée
84 g (3 oz) tomatoes
chilli powder
salt and pepper
barbecue seasoning
42 g (1½ oz) cheese
oregano
oil

Spread the dough in a lightly-greased pan. In a bowl mix the minced beef, green pepper, onion, tomato purée and tomatoes. Season well with chilli powder, salt, pepper and barbecue seasoning. Spread the Sloppy Joe sauce over the dough almost to the edge. Add cheese, more salt and pepper, oregano and oil. Cook in a hot oven, 230°C (450°F)/Gas 8, for 20 minutes.

The Colonel's Pizza

196 g (7 oz) basic dough
84 g (3 oz) tomato
oregano
56–84 g (2–3 oz) cooked chicken, thinly sliced
2 teaspoons mango chutney
1 teaspoon sultanas
paprika
salt and pepper
oil

Spread the dough evenly in a lightly-greased pan. Cover with tomato almost to the edge, and season with oregano. Spread the chicken slices over the pizza. Distribute mango chutney and sultanas and sprinkle generously with paprika. Add salt, pepper and oil. Bake at 230°C (450°F)/Gas 8 for 20 minutes.

King Edward's Pizza

In America they call this an Idaho pizza. It is clearly not traditional, but tastes delicious. I have made this pizza successfully using fresh, tinned and powdered potatoes and you can use any of your favourite toppings on it.

672 g (1½ lb) potatoes, peeled, boiled and mashed
1½ teaspoons salt
2 tablespoons butter
56 g (2 oz) Parmesan
1 egg, beaten
140 g (5 oz) tomato
56 g (2 oz) cheese
8 thin slices salami
28 g (1 oz) mushrooms
salt and pepper
oregano
oil

Mix the mashed potato with the salt, butter, Parmesan cheese and beaten egg. Press the mixture into a very lightly-floured 23-cm (9-in) pizza pan and give it a slightly raised edge by tapping the base all round about 1 cm (½ in) from the edge. Top with tomato, then cover with the sliced cheese, salami, and mushrooms. Add salt, pepper, oregano and oil. Bake at 230°C (450°F)/Gas 8 for 20 minutes.

Pizza Vesuvio

196 g (7 oz) basic dough
84 g (3 oz) tomato
28 g (1 oz) ricotta (or cottage cheese)
28 g (1 oz) mushrooms
1 hot green pepper
salt and pepper
oregano
oil
10 thin slices pepperoni
42 g (1½ oz) diced mozzarella

Before rolling the doughball into a circle, trim off about 14 g (½ oz) dough and, with a rolling pin, flatten it into a small circle about 10 cm (4 in) in diameter. Spread the remaining dough into a lightly-greased pan. In the centre make a 5-cm (2-in) circle of tomato. On top of this place the ricotta, sliced mushrooms and the chopped hot green pepper. Season with salt, pepper, oregano and a little oil. Cover with the small circle of dough, pressing it down well so that it sticks to the base. Cover the flat part of the dough with the remaining tomato. Place the pepperoni sausage in a circle around the foot of the 'mountain'. Sprinkle the mozzarella over the pepperoni and tomato. Add salt and pepper. The volcano can be lightly oiled or brushed with egg. Bake at 230°C (450°F)/Gas 8 for 20 minutes.

Pizza Siciliana

392 g (14 oz) basic dough
224 g (8 oz) tomatoes, pulped
112 g (4 oz) mozzarella
56 g (2 oz) ham
1–3 anchovies
3 baby artichokes
56 g (2 oz) pecorino

Spread the dough in a 23 × 30 cm (9 × 12 in) baking tray. Cover with peeled tomatoes which have been drained, seasoned and crushed. Slice the mozzarella and put on top of the tomato. Add the ham, broken into bite-sized pieces, anchovies, the baby artichokes cut in two, and lumps of pecorino cheese about the size of an olive. Add the olives, preferably

7 olives
garlic
oregano
salt and pepper
parsley

pitted. Add garlic, oregano, pepper and salt. Cook for 30 minutes at 230°C (450°F)/Gas 8. Lightly sprinkle with finely-chopped parsley before serving.

Note: Because of the increased length of cooking time, this is one of the pizzas for which it might be best to add the cheese at *mezzo cottura*, or halfway stage.

Variations

This pizza makes a pleasant change from round ones and is normally enough for two or three people, because it has a much thicker dough. It is excellent sliced into small pieces for parties.

If you're going to serve it cold, it helps if you increase the amount of tomato.

Pizza Ai Funghi

4 garlic cloves, crushed
6 tablespoons oil
224 g (8 oz) mushrooms
parsley
196 g (7 oz) basic dough
salt and pepper

Sauté the crushed garlic cloves in oil until light brown. Remove from oil. Shake off excess moisture from the mushrooms, slice and fry in oil for 5–7 minutes. Add the parsley and allow to cool. Meanwhile spread the dough evenly in a lightly-greased pan, then cover with the mushrooms almost to the edge. Add salt and a generous sprinkling of pepper. Bake for 20 minutes at 230°C (450°F)/Gas 8. Garnish with more chopped parsley.

The dough may be covered with a tablespoon of tomato.

Pizza San Terenzio

This recipe was concocted by an American girlfriend who when I met her liked neither Italy, nor pizza, nor me. She was converted!

196 g (7 oz) basic dough
84 g (3 oz) tomato
rosemary
basil
3 oysters
4 mussels
white wine
black pepper
finely-chopped shallots
14 g (½ oz) grated Parmesan
red pepper
oil
parsley
lemon juice

Spread the dough in a lightly-greased pan. Cover with tomato almost to the edge of the dough and sprinkle lightly with rosemary and basil. Thoroughly wash the oysters and mussels and put them in a saucepan with enough wine to cover, pepper and some of the shallot. Cook over a high heat, then drain and set aside. Sprinkle the pizza with the remaining shallots, grated Parmesan, a dash of red pepper and oil. Bake at 230°C (450°F)/Gas 8 for 10 minutes, then add the oysters and mussels and return to oven for a further 10 minutes. Garnish with parsley and a squeeze of lemon juice and, if you like, with a chopped hard-boiled egg.

Connoisseur Pizza

This pizza is named after a casino I know and should be very popular with your gambling friends.

196 g (7 oz) basic dough
84 g (3 oz) tomato
56 g (2 oz) red Danish style
  caviar
56 g (2 oz) black Danish
  style caviar
knob cottage cheese
1 olive
oil
lemon juice

Remove a small section from the dough. Roll out the rest and place it in a lightly-greased pan. Cover the base with tomato. Using the reserved piece of dough, roll out four thin strips and stretch them across the pizza to make 8 equal segments, pinching the ends together with the rim of the dough base. Spread the red and black roe in alternate sections. In the centre of the pizza, place a round knob of cottage cheese with an olive on top. Sprinkle oil on the pizza and bake in a hot oven, 230°C (450°F)/Gas 8, for 20 minutes. Remove and add a squeeze of lemon juice before serving.

Variations

Some friends of mine add an extra narrow section, making nine in all. This, filled with chopped fresh green pepper, represents the zero on a roulette wheel. You can have fun at a party by numbering the sections from 0 to 8 and, without letting your guests know where, secretly adding a knob of cottage cheese to one of the sections. Meanwhile your guests can bet on where the ball will have landed when the dish is served. You might call this variation Pizza Roulette.

If you are a real connoisseur you will, of course, want to use red and black Russian caviar instead of Danish.

Pizza Monica

This pizza takes its name from Monique, the waitress who first thought of this combination—and who married the *pizzaiolo* who first cooked it.

196 g (7 oz) basic dough
84 g (3 oz) tomato
1 tablespoon finely-chopped
  onion
1 teaspoon grated Parmesan
8 sardines in oil
8 leaves cooked spinach
salt and pepper
oil
lemon juice

Spread the dough evenly in a lightly-greased pan. Cover with tomato and sprinkle with chopped onion and grated Parmesan. Arrange the sardines spoke fashion on the pizza. Place the spinach in between the sardines and lightly season with salt and pepper. Brush the pizza with oil and bake at 230°C (450°F)/Gas 8 for 20 minutes. Sprinkle with lemon juice before serving.

Variations

An anchovy can be finely chopped and sprinkled over the spinach, or coiled round a stuffed green olive in the centre of the pizza.

Pizza 'Maria Stuarda'

This recipe was invented by Silvano Contiero, the *maitre d'hôtel* at the Hotel Excelsior in Naples, but he uses much smaller bases to make the pizza more suitable for a light snack.

196 g (7 oz) dough
84 g (3 oz) tomato
28 g (1 oz) mozzarella
salt and pepper
oil
28 g (1 oz) smoked salmon
freshly-ground black pepper

Begin by pinching off about 28 g (1 oz) of dough from your doughball (or you can use any spare dough you have to hand) before you stretch the remainder of the dough and spread it in a lightly-greased pan. Spread the tomato almost to the edge. Roll the spare piece of dough into three long strips between the palms of your hands. Stretch these across the pizza to divide it into six parts, pinching the ends to the rim of the dough base. Place the cheese in every other triangle, and sprinkle the whole pizza with salt, pepper, oil and oregano. Bake in a hot oven, 230°C (450°F)/Gas 8, for 20 minutes. Remove from the oven and place the slices of smoked salmon on the triangular sections where there is no cheese. Return to the oven for one minute. Remove, mill fresh pepper on to the smoked salmon, and serve.

Whitebait Pizza

This is the nearest we can get to pizza with *pescolini* in England. Frozen whitebait are good and allow us to enjoy this pizza throughout the year.

196 g (7 oz) dough
84 g (3 oz) tomato
56–84 g (2–3 oz) whitebait
salt and pepper
garlic clove
olive oil
lemon slices

Line a lightly-greased pan with the dough. Spread the tomato almost to the edge. Cover with whitebait, putting the largest ones on the outside. Generously season with salt and pepper and add some finely-chopped garlic if desired. Brush with oil and cook for 20 minutes at 230°C (450°F)/Gas 8. Serve with a slice of lemon.

Pizza con Cozze e Vongole

196 g (7 oz) dough
84 g (3 oz) tomato
5 cockles
8 mussels
chopped garlic
oil
salt
parsley
28 g (1 oz) cheese, diced
1 teaspoon Parmesan

Spread the dough evenly in a lightly-greased pan. Cover with tomato almost to the edge. Thoroughly scrub the cockles and mussels, and arrange them, opened, on the pizza. If preferred, these may be first mixed with chopped garlic, oil, salt and parsley. Add the diced cheese and sprinkle with Parmesan. Bake for 20 minutes at 230°C (450°F)/Gas 8. If you wish to be sure that the mussels don't turn hard and rubbery, add them at the halfway stage.

Pizza Parmentier

This pizza is named in honour of Antoine-Auguste Parmentier (1737–1817), who popularised the previously scorned potato in France.

196 g (7 oz) basic dough
84 g (3 oz) tomato
1 medium-sized potato
salt and pepper
28 g (1 oz) Parmesan
rosemary
oil

Spread the dough in a lightly-greased pan and cover with tomato almost to the edge. Scrape or peel the potato and cut into very thin slices—no more than 0.25 cm ($\frac{1}{8}$ in) thick. (You may boil the potato first if you wish, but there is no need to.) Arrange the slices on the tomato. Add salt, pepper and the grated Parmesan. Sprinkle with rosemary and add the oil. Bake for 20 minutes at 230°C (450°F)/Gas 8.

Small pieces of bacon or ham may be added, but it is best to place them in the gaps left by the potato, rather than on top.

Pizzetine

These are small pizzas, ideal for cocktail parties or a light snack at any time. The enriched dough (page 29) and the pizzetine dough (page 31) are particularly suitable for these delicacies. Roll out the dough until it is about 0.75 cm ($\frac{3}{8}$ in) thick. Cut out small circles of dough with a wine glass or tea cup. Allow them to rest for a few minutes—they will probably shrink a little. Grease a baking tray. Press the circles of dough with the palm of your hand so that they go back to their original size, then place them on the baking tray. Cover the dough circles almost to the edge with tomato, using a teaspoon to spread it. Then add any garnish of your choice—cheese, pitted olives and capers, anchovies, salami, gherkins, bite-sized pieces of fried bacon, chopped hard-boiled egg, tuna fish, prawns, sardines, Parmesan and rosemary or basil are just a few ideas. Or you can leave them as white pizza without the tomato, adding small pieces of fried bacon or sprigs of rosemary. Sprinkle with salt, pepper, oil and oregano and bake in a hot oven, 230°C (450°F)/Gas 8, for 10–15 minutes.

Pizza Frutta

Fresh fruit makes a delicious pizza, sweet or savoury; any fresh fruit I have ever come across goes perfectly on pizza. Enriched dough gives the best results and there's no need to use tomato. Slice the fruit very thinly, trying to retain its integral shape as you do so.

Place the pieces on the dough, so that they touch each other. Add a few sultanas, raisins and pine kernels if you have them. If not, split almonds will do. For a savoury pizza, sprinkle with mozzarella or Cheddar cheese, grated or finely diced. Add a little olive oil, plus a dash of cinnamon or nutmeg. Bake for 20 minutes at 230°C (450°F)/Gas 8. Enjoy your savoury fruit pizza!

For the sweet one, prepare the same way but instead of adding cheese, sprinkle 4 or 5 tablespoons caster sugar over the fruit. The sugar caramellises and you have a rich fruit pizza which, cut up in slices, will serve three or four people and can be eaten cold.

Pissaladière

Pissaladière could be called a French Provençal pizza although usually it has no mozzarella. It is particularly good with the enriched pizza dough (page 29) made with equal amounts of whole wheat and plain flour.

448 g (1 lb) onions
3–4 tablespoons olive oil
½ teaspoon crushed rosemary
224 g (½ lb) plum tomatoes, drained
salt and pepper
1 clove garlic
196 g (7 oz) dough
14 g (½ oz) Parmesan, grated
12 anchovies
12 black olives, pitted

First lightly cook the onions until soft in a covered frying pan with 3–4 tablespoons of olive oil and ½ teaspoon of crushed rosemary, taking care not to let them turn brown. Add the tomatoes, salt, pepper and a chopped clove of garlic.

Then spread the dough into a lightly-greased pan. Sprinkle the Parmesan over the dough base and cover with the prepared onion and tomato.

Place the anchovies over the filling in lattice fashion, and scatter the olives among the anchovies. Bake for 20 minutes at 230°C (450°F)/Gas 8.

Pizza Sardenaira (or Pizza all'Andrea or Pissadella)

Pizza Sardenaira is a Ligurian version of the Pissaladière. It is reputed to have been a favourite of the great Italian Admiral Andrea Doria, who is even credited with its invention. In Ventimiglia a version of Pissadella is simply to cover a large baking tray with dough, top the dough with tomatoes and a generous number of black olives, spike the dough with a few whole garlic cloves, and bake. When the pizza is taken from the oven, the garlic cloves are removed—having flavoured the dough in the cooking. Anchovy fillets are frequently included on a classic Pizza all'Andrea.

Michelle Vegetarian Pizza

This is a favourite at Renée Brittan's delightful Pizza Real in Las Palmas, Canary Islands. It is particularly popular with the Indian community and the local Canarios.

196 g (7 oz) dough
56 g (2 oz) tomato
1 onion
few capers
1 artichoke heart
few mushrooms
56 g (2 oz) cheese
½ green pepper
¼ red pepper
3 olives
salt and pepper
oregano
oil

Spread the dough in a lightly-greased pan. Spread the tomato almost to the edge. Cover the pizza with a layer of finely-sliced onion. Add a few capers, a tinned artichoke heart torn into pieces and a sprinkle of sliced mushrooms, according to taste. Distribute the cheese and decorate the top with thinly-sliced rings of green pepper, three strips of red pepper and three black olives. Season to taste and add a whiff of oregano and a dash of olive oil. Cook in a hot oven, 230°C (450°F)/Gas 8, for 20 minutes.

Pizza Rustica

In Italy, and particularly in Rome, many pizzerias are called 'Pizzeria Rustica'. These are usually take-away shops which use electric ovens to cook their pizzas. The *pizzetaro*, as he is known in the capital, bakes large slabs of pizza on standard rectangular bakers' trays. The cheese is sprinkled over the pizza just before it finishes cooking, and the dough makes a crisp crackling noise as the *pizzetaro* lifts it at one corner to see if it is baked to perfection. Pizza Rustica is sold by weight—usually by the 'etto', which is approximately 112 g ($\frac{1}{4}$ lb)—and the clever *pizzetaro* tries to sell it as soon as possible before much of the weight evaporates through cooling!

But the true Pizza Rustica is what we would call a double-crusted pizza. This is not really pizza as we know it and some varieties of Pizza Rustica are very heavy, much as our Christmas pudding is. They are often made at festive seasons, particularly at Easter, and frequently are filled with sweet ingredients. In the old days the preparation could last for several days.

Here are two recipes for authentic double-crusted pizzas which you might like to try. The variations, as usual, are enormous! The traditional recipe for a Pizza Rustica calls for short pastry, but today the basic pizza dough or an enriched dough is often used. If you are using the basic dough for this pizza, I recommend that you add 14 g ($\frac{1}{2}$ oz) lard to the dough before kneading.

Pizza Rustica

392 (14 oz) basic dough
280 g (10 oz) ricotta
4 eggs, beaten
84 g (3 oz) Parmesan
parsley, chopped
salt
196 g (7 oz) mozzarella
140 g (5 oz) smoked Provola
  or Austrian smoked cheese
112 g (4 oz) salami or ham
pepper

Divide the dough into two pieces, one slightly larger than the other, and roll into two discs. Place the larger disc in a well-greased 23-cm (9-in) pie tin with the edges of the dough covering the top of the tin.

In a mixing bowl beat the ricotta with a fork. Add the egg, reserving a little of it, and beat until the mixture becomes like a paste. Add the grated Parmesan, the chopped parsley, a pinch of salt and mix well.

Cut the mozzarella, smoked cheese and salami into small chunks, add pepper, and mix in with the paste. Spread the mixture on to the dough in the pie tin, and cover with the smaller disc of dough, crimping the edges together. Any spare trimmings can be rolled into a thin strip and laid decoratively on the surface. Brush the remaining egg lightly over the top and bake at 190°C (375°F)/Gas 5 for about one hour or until the top becomes brown. Remove from the tin, allow to cool and serve.

Variations

A fresh sausage or two may be added to the filling if desired. The Italians add the sausage in winter.

In Lecce, where the Pizza Rustica is famous, sautéd onions, tomatoes and anchovies are used in the filling.

In some parts of Italy the egg yolks are beaten with the other ingredients and the whites are beaten until stiff and then folded in. A tablespoon of sultanas, a pinch of nutmeg and 2 hard-boiled eggs are added in this version.

Pizza di Scarola

This is a traditional pizza for Christmas Eve in some parts of Italy and, without the anchovies, is a favourite of Sophia Loren. Scarola is a frilly, crisp endive, not easily found in England, but lettuce can be used as a substitute.

*4 small heads Batavian
  endive or cos lettuce
2 tablespoons capers
1 tablespoon pine kernels
1 tablespoon sultanas
6 pitted black olives
5 anchovies (optional)
olive oil
1 clove garlic
392 g (14 oz) basic dough*

Thoroughly wash the lettuce, boil for a few minutes in salty water, drain and put to one side. Gently heat the capers, pine kernels, sultanas, olives and anchovies in olive oil to which a clove of garlic has been added. After 10 minutes add the lettuce, turning the leaves in the hot oil. Take off the heat and allow to cool; this will improve the flavour.

Divide the dough in two. Spread the large piece of dough in a lightly-greased 23-cm (9-in) pie tin and add the filling, which should be well drained of oil. Place the smaller disc of dough over the filling and crimp the edge. Lightly sprinkle the top with oil, allow to rest in a warm place for 15 minutes, and then bake at 230°C (450°F)/Gas 8 for 20 minutes. Serve hot, just warm, or cold.

Dried cod makes a nice addition to the filling.

Frizza Pizza

*196 g (7 oz) frizza dough
  (page 31)
oil
56 g (2 oz) mozzarella
other ingredients as desired*

Roll out the dough and cut out a circle the size of your frying pan. Heat just enough oil in the pan to cover the dough disc. Prick the surface of the dough with a fork, then fry the disc on one side until golden brown. Turn it over, add the cheese and your chosen topping almost to the edge and cover the pan. Cook for 4–5 minutes until the cheese is melted and the underside is brown. Serve at once.

Variations

To make a frizza Neapolitan style, divide the dough in two and roll into 2 thin circles. Put cheese, mortadella or ham, salt, pepper and oregano on one dough disc. Cover with the second dough disc and pinch the edges together very firmly. Deep fry in hot oil for 2–3 minutes.

You might like to make this in the shape of a pasty, well sealed and filled with sugared banana (*banazza*) or stewed apple (*appleazza*).

Pizza al Formaggio

There are many pizzas similar to this one, where the ingredients are cooked in with the dough rather than spread on the surface. While they are not, perhaps, 'pizzas' as we know them, but more like flavoured bread or cake, they have a pleasing subtle flavour. This one makes a delightful cheesy pizza.

56 g (2 oz) Parmesan
56 g (2 oz) pecorino
84 g (3 oz) Gruyère or
  provolone
2 eggs
salt
392 g (14 oz) dough
olive oil
coarse salt
pinch rosemary

Grate one-third of the Parmesan, pecorino and Gruyère and cut the rest of the cheese into small cubes. Beat the eggs and add the cheese and a pinch of salt. Knead well into the dough (which should have risen once) and allow to rest, covered with a damp cloth, until it starts to rise again.

Oil a 23-cm (9-in) pizza pan or flan dish and spread the dough so that it is about 2.5 cm (1 in) thick. Sprinkle with coarse salt, oil and a little rosemary. Bake at 230°C (450°F)/Gas 8 for 30 minutes. Cut into portions and serve hot or cold.

Focaccia

This is a Genoese version of pizza which is also popular in Southern Italy. The Italians have a saying *'render pane per focaccia'* which means 'to give bread for focaccia' or tit for tat, which shows how close focaccia is to the staff of life.

To make a Focaccia alla Salvia (a kind of sage bread) knead 2 teaspoons sage into 392 g (14 oz) dough. Spread the dough in a lightly-greased 23-cm (9-in) pan, so that it is about 2.5 cm (1 in) thick. Allow to rest for 15 minutes, then prick the surface with a fork, sprinkle with olive oil and a generous pinch of coarse salt and bake in a moderate oven—200°C (400°F)/Gas 6—for 30 minutes. This tasty bread can be eaten hot or cold.

Pizza di Scamorza

I sometimes wince when I see how bread is used to make concoctions which masquerade under the name of pizza. However, this recipe from Naples uses, believe it or not, slices of tin loaf!

lard or butter
6 slices bread
224 g (8 oz) mozzarella
salt
basil or parsley
1 egg, beaten
pepper
2 or 3 peeled tomatoes
  (optional)
2 anchovies

Grease a baking tray with fat and place the slices of bread on it so that they cover the surface completely. Cover with thinly-sliced mozzarella, sprinkle with salt and the basil or parsley, and brush with the beaten egg. Season with pepper and, if you are using them, add the tomatoes—but be sure you have drained them well or they will make the bread soggy. Place in an oven preheated to 230°C (450°F)/Gas 8. Add the anchovies, split, after 15 minutes, and then cook for a further five minutes. The bread should be crispy and the topping golden brown.

Pizza al Metro

Any of the recipes you find in this book can be used to make *pizza al metro* or pizza by the yard. The name comes from an enormous pizzeria—the Al Metro—seating over 1,000 at Vico Equense between Naples and Sorrento. When you order you simply tell the waiter how many centimetres of pizza you want and the chef measures it accordingly. On my last visit to Vico Equense I stopped at the village's tiny photography shop, which is run by painter Charles Lincar. On hearing I was going to visit the Pizzeria Al Metro he composed a poem on the spot for me to hand to Don Gigino, the owner:

A pizza
La facevano i romani
La mangiavano i Borboni
Poi la fece don Gigino
Con la pala ed il metrone.

Which is an ode saying that Don Gigino is following in the steps of the Romans and the Bourbons with the addition of his pizza metre.

In the Pizzeria Al Metro three huge ovens looking more like blast furnaces turn out the desired number of centimetres of pizza in a variety of flavours. If you wish to serve pizza 'al Metro' at home—and it's a good party idea—you will need a big oven and a long dish on which to put the pizza. Or you can cook two or more rectangular pizzas about 20 cm (8 in) wide, cut the crusts off at one end and join the two pizzas together to make one long one.

A Zodiac of Pizzas

I REMEMBER SITTING late one night, shortly after the first PizzaExpress opened, over a bottle of Chianti and a couple of Napoletanas with a thin, wild-eyed man who turned out to be an astrologer. He spoke at length, and fascinatingly, of how the stars influence almost everything we do. Almost jokingly I asked him if the stars influence what we eat and if those born under the various signs of the zodiac are interested in particular flavours. 'Of course,' he replied, and began to explain.

As a result of that conversation I have, from time to time over the years, created special pizzas with the appropriate ingredients to give to friends on their birthdays. It was great fun and though some contested my choice, the pizzas were always popular.

Whether or not you believe in astrology, you'll find here another dozen ideas for good pizzas which are delicious at any time. Honour a friend's anniversary with one, or just make them for fun.

Incidentally, many customers have asked me if there is such a thing as an aphrodisiac pizza. Well, I have my own ideas about that and you'll find the answer in this section.

Pages 72–3 : An elegant collection of pizzas at Coptic Street. Clockwise from back : Whitebait (62), Giardiniera (53), Prawn (52), Con Cozze e Vongole (63), Calzone (56), Marinara (49), Siciliana (59), Four Seasons (49), Connoisseur (61). In the middle: Mozzarella and Tomato Salad (90) and, behind, a Capricciosa (50).

Aries (March 21–April 20)
Ruler: Mars

Aries people tend to be fairly down-to-earth in their tastes; the ruling planet suggests that the chosen food should be substantial, though not necessarily crude. This pizza is hearty but interesting, with its oriental overtones.

Pizza Imam Byeldu (The Sultan Swooned)

Tradition has it that a Turkish sultan fainted with delight when confronted with an exquisitely prepared dish of aubergines. I suggest that he may have reacted with a more practical appreciation had he been served the following pizza.

196 g (7 oz) basic dough
56 g (2 oz) tomato
1 small aubergine (about 224 g (8 oz))
oil
56 g (2 oz) cheese, cubed
pine nuts
olives
salt

Spread the dough in a lightly-greased pan. Make sure your tomato sauce is very well flavoured with garlic, bay and parsley. Spread it on the dough. Peel the aubergine if you like, though it isn't necessary. Cut it into *very* thin slices and brown them quickly in hot oil. Arrange the slices attractively in a wheel on top of the tomato. Sprinkle with the cubed cheese (mozzarella, Bel Paese or Port Salut) and decorate with pine nuts and olives. Add salt and a sprinkle of good oil. Cook for 20 minutes at 230°C (450°F)/Gas 8.

Taurus (April 21–May 20)
Ruler: Venus

People born under this sign are regarded as those most likely to enjoy a vegetarian diet. The prevailing influence of Venus suggests sexuality and fertility, which can be hinted at by the use of seedy fruits or vegetables. Green is the appropriate colour.

The Taurus

196 g (7 oz) whole wheat dough
56 g (2 oz) onions
oil
224 g (8 oz) fresh tomatoes
112 g (4 oz) courgettes
basil (if available) or parsley
olives
capers
56 g (2 oz) Parmesan
salt

Make sure the whole wheat dough is rolled very thin and spread it in a lightly-greased pan. Finely chop the onions and melt them in a little hot oil for about 15 minutes. Cover the pan so that they cannot brown or fry. Roughly chop the tomatoes and slice the courgettes into small pieces. Spread the softened onions on the dough; cover with circles of courgette and sprinkle with plenty of basil or parsley. Add the tomatoes. Arrange the olives and scatter capers on top. Sprinkle with cheese, salt and oil and cook at 230°C (450°F)/Gas 8 for 20 minutes.

Gemini (May 21–June 20)
Ruler: Mercury

The dual-natured Geminian is not particularly decisive in his food taste, but will enjoy an unexpected novelty. The presence of Mercury suggests fun and lightness, so work on a variation of the classic contrast between meat and fruit.

The Twin Pizza

196 g (7 oz) basic dough
56 g (2 oz) tomato
1 garlic clove
56 g (2 oz) onions (softened in oil)
1 small can tuna
capers
2 firm pears
6 green olives
4 small prunes (soaked)
oregano
salt
oil

Line the bottom of the pizza pan with dough. Spread the tomato, mixed with a crushed garlic clove, on one half of the dough; spread the softened onions on the other half. Flake the tuna and arrange it on top of the tomato, then decorate with a generous sprinkle of capers. Peel and dice the pears, arrange them on the onions and decorate with the olives and the prunes. Sprinkle with oregano, salt and oil and cook at 230°C (450°F)/Gas 8 for 20 minutes.

Cancer (June 21–July 21)
Ruler: Moon

Oddly, Cancerians are not particularly fond of seafood, but they do have a good appetite and like a lot of food. Try this variation on the bacon pizza. A true Cancerian will eat the entire pizza and probably ask for another!

The One-man Pizza

196 g (7 oz) basic dough
56 g (2 oz) bacon
56 g (2 oz) tomato
1 tablespoon mango chutney
28 g (1 oz) cheese, cubed
oil
1 egg
1 teaspoon Parmesan cheese (or very finely-grated dry Cheddar)
oregano

Spread the dough in a lightly-greased pan. With the blunt edge of a knife, stretch one rasher of bacon. Cut the rest into small pieces. Spread the tomato on the dough, and arrange the stretched rasher in a circle (on its edge) in the centre. Scatter the chopped bacon pieces around it and spread the chutney and the cheese among them. Sprinkle with oil. Bake at 230°C (450°F)/Gas 8 for 10 minutes, then break the egg in the circle of bacon and cover it with Parmesan cheese. Add more oil and oregano and return to the oven for another 5 or 10 minutes.

Leo (July 22–August 21)
Ruler: Sun

Leos are, traditionally, the heroes of the Zodiac, the leaders, the golden boys and girls; they love luxury and excellence and appreciate food of the highest quality. Do not try to be clever with them, but simply bake the best of classic Italian pizzas.

A Rich Pizza

FOR THE DOUGH:
*14 g (¼ oz) fresh yeast or 2
  level teaspoons dried yeast*
140 g (5 oz) flour
1 teaspoon salt
56 g (2 oz) butter
1 egg, beaten
FOR THE FILLING:
56 g (2 oz) tomato
56 g (2 oz) mozzarella
2 anchovy fillets
olives
oregano
salt
oil

Dissolve the yeast in a little tepid water. Sift the flour and salt. Rub in the butter until the mixture resembles fine crumbs. Add the yeast mixture and a little of the beaten egg. Mix to a dough, adding more egg if necessary. Knead until smooth and elastic and leave to rise for an hour.

Preheat the oven to 230°C (450°F)/Gas 8 and spread the dough in a lightly-greased pan. Cover with tomato sauce, highly seasoned, and then the cubed cheese. Soak the anchovy fillets in a little milk, drain and divide them lengthwise. Arrange the anchovies on the cheese in a lattice pattern, putting an olive in each square or division. Sprinkle with oregano, a little salt and oil. Bake for 20 minutes.

Essentially this is the classic Neapolitan pizza, but made into a Leo complement with the delicious crisp base.

Virgo (August 22–September 21)
Ruler: Mercury

Virgos are, it seems, famous for their fastidiousness and discrimination—which can also make them finicky and dubious about the unfamiliar. So try this interesting combination.

Chicken Pizza

196 g (7 oz) basic dough
56 g (2 oz) tomato
*112 g (4 oz) cold, cooked
  chicken*
*56 g (2 oz) sweet corn
  (canned or frozen, but not
  'creamed-style')*
dozen stuffed green olives
56 g (2 oz) cheese
oil
oregano

Spread the dough in a lightly-greased pan and top with tomato. Cut the chicken into chunky pieces and arrange on the tomato. Sprinkle sweetcorn all over the surface and add the olives. Cover the chicken pieces with grated cheese and a little oil. Be sure that all the chicken pieces are well covered, or they will dry out when the pizza cooks, and be unappetizing. Add oregano and other herbs to taste, and bake at 230°C (450°F)/Gas 8 for 20 minutes.

Libra (September 22–October 22)
Ruler: Venus

Librans are charming, sensual and appreciate the finer things of the table. The presence of Venus suggests that thoughts might be directed to aphrodisiac possibilities. Since a dinner party for a Libran will be elegant, here is a nice variation on the pizza which makes an ideal first course. The recipe will make 2 small pizzas.

The Venus

FOR THE DOUGH:
112 g (4 oz) self-raising flour
¼ teaspoon salt
84 g (3 oz) butter
lemon juice
Marsala
FOR THE FILLING:
112 g (4 oz) shellfish
(prawns, crab, lobster, etc.)
olive oil
lemon juice
fennel
salt and pepper
56 g (2 oz) tomato
truffles or capers
56 g (2 oz) Parmesan

Sift flour and salt; cut in the butter, add a few drops of lemon juice and make into dough with as much Marsala as you need to achieve a smooth and supple doughball. Chill.

Preheat the oven to 200°C (400°F)/Gas 6. Marinate the fish in 2 parts oil mixed with 1 part lemon juice, fennel and seasoning. Roll out the pastry and cut two 12.5-cm (5-in) circles. Spread them with tomato. Drain the fish and arrange it on top of the tomato. Add sliced truffles (or capers) and sprinkle with cheese. Pour about a tablespoonful of the marinade over the pizza and bake for 12 minutes.

Scorpio (October 23–November 21)
Ruler: Mars

Perhaps no one will appreciate a pizza more than a person born under this sign. Scorpio is the sign of bakers, and anything cooked in an oven will be happily received. They are also, I am told, greedy.

The Gourmandizer's Pizza

196 g (7 oz) basic dough
56 g (2 oz) fresh tomatoes, crushed
sausage (see method)
56 g (2 oz) onion
1 tomato, sliced
56 g (2 oz) mushrooms
fresh sage

Lightly grease the pizza pan and line with the dough. Spread the crushed tomato, well seasoned, on the dough. For the sausage, you can add ordinary sausage cut into 1-cm (½-in) slices, whole tiny sausages, sliced canned frankfurters or sausagemeat, seasoned and rolled into tiny balls and quickly fried in a little oil. Scatter finely-sliced raw onion and the tomato slices among the sausages, then add the mushrooms. Sprinkle with chopped fresh sage and cook at 230°C (450°F)/Gas 8 for 20 minutes.

Sagittarius (November 22–December 20)
Ruler: Jupiter

Sagittarians are usually active, out-going, and interested in outdoor pursuits. Something suggestive of the outdoors and of the autumnal season is appropriate. The addition of chestnuts in this recipe comes from Corsica, where there are good pizzas and some of the most beautiful chestnut woods in Europe.

An Autumn Pizza

112 g (4 oz) chestnuts
196 g (7 oz) basic dough
56 g (2 oz) tomato
1 onion
2 stalks celery
oil
1 green pepper
56 g (2 oz) cheese
salt

The chestnuts must be skinned, a tedious business. Slit them on their round side and roast them for 10 minutes in the preheating oven, while you prepare the dough and the pizza pan. They should then be easy to skin. Spread the dough in the pan and cover with tomato almost to the edge. Finely chop the onion, slice the celery and soften them together in oil over a low heat. When soft, spread the celery and onion over the tomato. Slice the pepper into very thin rings and arrange on top. Crush the chestnuts and add them to the pizza together with the cheese, salt and a sprinkling of oil. Bake in a hot oven, 230°C (450°F)/Gas 8, for 20 minutes.

Variations
You can also add mushrooms and some pieces of cold, cooked game bird. If you do use cooked meat, remember to cover it with the cheese or a liberal amount of oil so that it doesn't dry out with further cooking.

Small, whole onions make a nice change: peel and parboil them for 10 minutes before you add them to the pizza.

Capricorn (December 21–January 19)
Ruler: Saturn

These can be very jolly people and great fun, though they often have a serious side and are very sincere. Ironically, the festive food associated with this time of the year is not really suitable to the Capricornian. But most people will welcome a simple, uncomplicated pizza among the Christmas abundance.

A Christmas Pizza

196 g (7 oz) basic dough
56 g (2 oz) tomato
2 garlic cloves
56 g (2 oz) cooked ham
black olives
herbs

Lightly grease the pizza pan and line with the dough. Spread the tomato on the dough and sprinkle with finely-chopped garlic. Cut the ham into strips and arrange on the tomato. Throw olives casually on top. Add herbs to taste and cook in a hot oven, 230°C (450°F)/Gas 8 for 20 minutes.

Aquarius (January 20–February 18)
Ruler: Saturn

Charm, a delight in experiment, social ease and intuition characterise Aquarians. Often they are vegetarian and do not appreciate an excess of lavishness. They are influenced by Uranus (one of Saturn's planets), which also suggests an interest in simple food.

Spinach Pizza

196 g (7 oz) whole wheat dough
448 g (1 lb) spinach
nutmeg
salt and pepper
56 g (2 oz) walnuts, chopped
56 g (2 oz) Parmesan

Spread the dough in a lightly-greased pan. Wash spinach carefully, removing faded bits and thick stalks. Cover and cook, with a little salt, in the water clinging to it. Drain well and chop, adding a generous grate of nutmeg, pepper, salt and the chopped walnuts. Spread on the dough and sprinkle with Parmesan cheese. Bake for 20 minutes at 230°C (450°F)/Gas 8.

For variety, add a poached egg to the centre of the pizza before serving.

Pisces (February 19–March 20)
Ruler: Jupiter and Neptune

Pisceans are the most elusive characters, so turning more to the influence of Neptune we discover that the appropriate flavours are those associated with Italy, especially garlic, bay and basil. Combine these with a touch of fish for a pizza which is well-suited to a Piscean.

Pizza Pizzaiolo

196 g (7 oz) basic dough
112 g (4 oz) tomato sauce
3 anchovies
1 small can tuna
1 can sardines
few black olives
56 g (2 oz) Parmesan
lemon wedges to garnish

Lightly grease the pizza pan and line with the dough. Make up a rich tomato sauce (page 34) with onions, garlic, tomatoes, a little white wine, some red wine, tomato purée and plenty of parsley and basil. Incorporate 3 chopped anchovy fillets and spread thickly on the dough. Arrange the flaked tuna and sardines on top, adding black olives and the cheese. Bake 20 minutes at 230°C (450°F)/Gas 8 and serve with a wedge of lemon.

A Round-up of Italian Pizzas

HEN I TOLD culinary minded friends I was preparing this book on pizza they laughingly said it should be quite easy to write a book of three pages. There are an enormous number of variations on the pizza, many of them obscure and known only in certain regions of Italy and elsewhere. I list some of them here, by way of reference. (Should you require detailed recipes I shall be happy to supply them.) You will notice that many of them are double-crusted pizzas, for which I know no real equivalent in the UK.

Aglio e Olio: Garlic, oil, oregano and pepper if desired. From Naples.

Aglio Olio e Pomodoro: Another Neapolitan pizza, topped with tomatoes cooked in garlic oil and oregano.

Ai Cecinielli: Cecinielli is a small fish, 2–3 cm in length, of the anchovy family. It is not found in England. This is a Neapolitan pizza, which uses cecinielli, a crushed garlic clove and oregano.

Alla Romana: A Margherita Bianca topped with boned, salted anchovies. From Naples.

Alle Alici Fresche: From Naples, this pizza is topped with fresh anchovies, garlic and oil.

Alle Cozze: Pizza with a simple topping of mussels, chopped garlic, pepper, and oregano or parsley.

Anconetana: Parmesan, pecorino, Gruyère and eggs, all kneaded into the dough. No topping.

Barese: Small pizzas made with potato dough, fried, topped and baked in an oven for 10 minutes.

81

Bellanapoli: A Neapolitan concoction, divided into 5 sections: capers, black olives and anchovy; cockles; mussels; mushrooms in oil; 5 artichokes in oil. Place a rosette of mozzarella in the centre, at *mezzo cottura*.

Bracciano: An 'Easter pizza' topped with sugar, rosolio of citrus, vanilla, cinnamon and chocolate.

Calabrese: Double-crusted pizza with a filling of tomatoes, tuna, olives, capers and anchovies.

Calzuncieddi: Small calzone, fried in oil, from Puglia.

Campagnola: Pecorino, dolce latte, sugar, eggs and lemon mixed into the dough. No topping.

Campofranco: A double-crusted pizza using enriched dough and topped with ham, tomato, mozzarella, Parmesan, basil.

Cicciole e Uvetta: A Calabrian pizza, ring-shaped, with 'crackling' and sultanas.

Civitavecchia: A sweet pizza—requiring days of preparation—using sugar, ricotta, cinnamon, aniseeds soaked in Chianti and eggs.

Contadina: Topping of thin slices of mozzarella and provolone, sautéd onions, and anchovies; covered with tomato *'casalinga'*.

Cosacca: Another pizza from Naples. Use double the usual quantity of tomatoes and add 28 g (1 oz) grated Parmesan.

Farina Gialla: From Umbria, this pizza is made from maize flour, eggs, Parmesan and black truffles.

Frattese: A simple, classic pizza: just oil, cheese and tomato.

Isolana: Topping of tomatoes, anchovies, black olives, capers, basil, and oregano; half a dozen cloves of unpeeled garlic are placed upright in the topping.

Maiyu: Double-crusted, this pizza is a speciality from Ardore in Calabria. It is topped with ricotta, 'crackling', hard-boiled eggs, mozzarella and salami or ham.

Marche: A form of cheese pizza with no topping.

Noce e Canditi: A walnut and candied peel pie from Liguria, made from powdered walnuts, eggs, candied peel and chocolate, shaped like a pizza and eaten cold.

Pasqualino: This pizza, from Naples, is divided into 4 sections, each of which has its own name: Posillipo—prawns and calamares; Cassuola—fresh anchovy and tomatoes; Margherita—mozzarella, tomatoes and basil; and Alla

Romana—mozzarella, anchovy, basil and pepper. Serve with a hard-boiled egg in the centre.

Piedina di Romagna: A type of focaccia cooked on a special fire stone known as a *'testo'*.

Pitta alla Calabrese: Double-crusted, with ricotta, 'crackling', ham, cacciocavallo cheese, and hard-boiled eggs.

Pitta Chicculiata: *See* Calabrese.

Pitta Inchiusa: Double-crusted pizza filled with 'crackling', from Calabria. Cooked spinach, other greens or fresh sardines cooked in tomato may be substituted for the 'crackling'.

Pizza con la Ricotta: Double-crusted, from Calabria, with ham, eggs, ricotta, grated pecorino and parsley.

Pizza con la Porpa: With pitted olives, from Genoa.

Pizzi di Pasqua alla Romana: An Easter pizza from Rome, really more like a cake, with eggs, cinnamon, ricotta and lemon peel.

Polenta: Common in northern Italy, this pizza is made with a special base of corn meal (polenta).

Pomodoro e Formaggio: The dough is first rubbed with lard, then topped with canned and fresh tomatoes, Parmesan and basil or parsley.

Puddica: A form of focaccia from Puglia, made with garlic and fresh tomatoes, and often eaten in Bari with seafood delicacies.

Pugliese: A double-crusted pizza with onions, olives, tomatoes and anchovies.

Rieti: An Easter pizza with sugar, butter, cinnamon and lemon peel.

Sfinciuni di Santu Vitu: There are many types of Sfinciuni, a Palerman speciality. This one, with tomatoes, onions and sardines, is made by the nuns from the convent of Santu Vitu in Palermo.

Sfrizzoli: A Roman pizza with sugar, eggs, 'crackling' and lemon peel.

Spiziosa: Similar to a small fried calzone, filled with mozzarella and anchovy.

Sugna e Parmigiano: Neapolitans make this by rubbing lard on to the dough base, then topping it with grated Parmesan, a generous amount of basil or parsley, and salt and pepper.

Terni: An Easter pizza with pecorino cheese.

Uova e Cipolle: Double-crusted pizza, with lightly sautéd onion, hard-boiled eggs and parsley.

Pizza e Vino

PIZZA IS A DISH which does not demand the accompaniment of great wines, though if you have a grand *cru* in your cellar, why not use the energy you have expended on your pizza as an excuse to treat yourself to something special! Normally, an honest *vino da pasto*, as the Italians call their simple table wines, will be sufficient, but see you have plenty of it. Pizza is a convivial dish and you and your guests will want to quaff several glasses while it is cooking, as well as during and after the meal. If the wine is an inexpensive red, it does no harm to cool it slightly before serving. White wine and any beer you provide should always be chilled. A good Chianti is excellent with pizza; it should be a dry, roughish, prickly wine. Some exporters deliberately mellow their Chianti for the British market. Try to avoid these. Ask your merchant for a Chianti with a real bite to it.

Valpolicella and Frascati are the other wines which I have always found go well with any pizza. If you are having a celebration, a dry Asti Spumante helps to make it a memorable occasion, or you can splurge and enjoy the delights of a good champagne. Dom Perignon? Why not?

In America, and indeed in Italy too, beer is a very popular drink with pizza. Knowing how well the two go together, I contacted Italy's largest brewer, Birra Peroni, for the United Kingdom agency. As a result we are now importers and distributors of the excellent Nastro Azzurro. Especially good with pizza, it is one of the strongest and best European beers, made, like the best Italian pizza, in Naples. But any beer goes down well. In keeping with the simple traditions of pizza, which is so often eaten with the fingers, don't be afraid to offer beer as it comes—in the can.

For an aperitif you can't beat a Campari and soda, a Punt ē Mes or any red or white dry vermouth with lots of ice and a slice of lemon.

To follow a pizza my own preference is a grappa, from northern Italy. It is made from the skins of pressed grapes and has a very pronounced flavour. Buy a good quality brand such as Nardini or Da Ponte, or it is liable to taste like lighter fuel.

Strega liqueur, flavoured with herbs, makes a good digestif (and incidentally, a good aperitif when served on the rocks) as do the Italian brandies such as Stock and Vecchia Romagna. Perhaps the most intriguing liqueur to follow the pizza, and one which will delight your guests, is sambuca, a traditional 42°-proof aniseed-based liqueur, produced by Molinari at Civitavecchia. It is usually served with a couple of roasted coffee beans, known as 'flies'. In an Italian restaurant it is sometimes a gentle joust to see if you can obtain a sambuca free from the proprietor. Much depends on whether you order it before or after asking for the bill.

On pages 95–6, you will find a table containing suggestions as to what kind of drink to serve with which pizza. But above all else, remember that pizza goes well with almost any libation, whether an offering to Bacchus or not. Simply see that what you do serve comes in copious quantities—and may it be red!

Pizza Parties

PIZZA MAKES AN excellent theme for a party; suitably sliced, the pieces can be passed around on trays and are easy to eat with your fingers. You can make a variety of toppings so that all tastes are satisfied and all aversions avoided. Back up the pizza with some crisp salads, and garlic bread, and serve fruit or individual fruit mousses to follow. Wine is essential. Since pizzas are aromatic and richly flavoured, they tend not to marry with very fine wines; offer a sound Italian red or white wine, perhaps decanted into big jugs; and have a supply of Coke and beer in the fridge.

The easiest way to throw a pizza party, especially an impromptu one, is to collect the pizzas from your local pizzeria. Before you leave to get them, set the oven to full heat. Pizzas are always best straight from the original oven—in fact pizza experts claim this is the only way to enjoy them. But they do spring back to life in the most gratifying way if they are popped into a hot oven for a moment or two before serving. Add a sprinkle of olive oil to them when they come out of your oven, to make them glisten. Don't use any old lamp oil, or the delicate flavours contrived in the pizzeria will be ruined.

Watching people buy pizzas from the take-away counters at Pizza-Express, I have sometimes wondered what has happened to the pizzas as they are taken off to various parts of London and the country. I have seen all sorts of people standing waiting for their pizza to cook and as soon as they receive it in a box clearly marked 'Please keep level', they fling it into their briefcase or carrier bag and rush off before they can be stopped. The gooey mess that will have slunk to the bottom of the bag when they open it up doesn't bear thinking about. So keep them on the level!

It is more than likely that, between the pizzeria and your oven, the pizza will have dried a little and solidified a bit, a process which will continue with reheating. This doesn't matter very much at all; in fact for

87

a party it is an advantage because the pizza is much easier to eat with your fingers when it is in this condition, as it does not flop about.

The easiest way to serve pizzas is to cut them up into pieces, set them on plates and either hand them round or let the people help themselves. A pizza brought in from a pizzeria can be cut up into little slivers which make excellent canapés; if this is your intention, order a basically simple pizza, such as the Margherita, a mushroom or salami. These will cut easily without being too gooey. Also, with simple pizzas you can add your own extra goodies on top before the reheating: Danish or Russian caviar for an impressive effect; a slice of egg with anchovy; bacon curls; prawns; cocktail onions . . . the list is endless, the permutations enormous and I hope the preceding recipes will give you some ideas. One warning: be careful with the anchovies, because some people cannot bear them, or anything that has even been near them. Others cannot deal with black olives—which I find a great shame.

Making your own pizzas for a party does, of course, demand a little pre-planning and work beforehand, but of all hot foods to serve to a throng of people, pizza is certainly the easiest. The first thing to think about is quantities. Some people will eat as much pizza as they can see; others will be content with one slice—say a third or a quarter of a 23-cm (9-in) pizza. Erring on the generous side, I would suggest you calculate each person will eat half a standard pizza. So for twelve people you would make six pizzas. If it is your intention that your guests should eat their slice of pizza from a plate, with some salad, then divide the pies into quarters for service. If the guests are to help themselves at will, divide each pizza into eight.

Before your guests arrive, make the dough, roll it out and fill your pizza pans. Give the dough a light brush of oil and leave the pans in a cool place covered with a cloth—they will come to no harm. Then prepare the ingredients you are going to use, placing them in individual basins. Allow three-quarters of an hour from preparation to service; heat the oven first and by the time you have topped the pizzas, the oven will be hot enough to start cooking.

Place one pizza on the top shelf and a second on the shelf below, set on the next rack. By the time the top pizza is cooked, the second can be moved to the top shelf for a few minutes to complete its cooking, and the third pizza put in the oven. Buffet parties are not occasions when everyone wants to eat at exactly the same time, and with all the fun of serving going on and the cries of delight from your guests, the time lag will barely be noticed.

If you are making six pizzas, I suggest that one be richly aromatic in the traditional style—a Napoletana with olives and anchovies; a second might have a meat content (bacon, pepperoni, sausage of some kind); and a third should be vegetarian. The arrangement of the ingredients may need to be slightly adjusted for your party pizza, so that every slice will contain a portion of all the ingredients. Be careful not to overload the topping, and put the weightier ingredients towards the edge. Balancing an olive on a triangular tip of pizza at a party is no easy task.

An alternative method is to make your pizzas on 25-cm (10-in) square oven plates—each will divide into nine substantial pieces, and two of this size will serve each guest very adequately.

You can also make smaller pizzas, individual ones even, but this must depend on the size of your oven. An ordinary 25-cm (10-in) oven plate will take three 12.5-cm (5-in) pizzas or four smaller ones; if you make them any smaller, you are producing canapés—not a substantial main course, but nevertheless delightful for the right occasion. The dough for these can be stamped out with a tea cup or wine glass as I have described under Pizzetine (page 63).

If you are giving a party to celebrate a particular occasion, pizza is a good solution because it's very adaptable. For instance, for a children's party make pizza bambino. Cut puff pastry or thinly-rolled dough with a gingerbread-man mould and cover the individual bases with tomato sauce (page 34). Chop a black olive to make two eyes, a nose and a mouth, and use tiny pieces of fresh green pepper for buttons on the bambino's coat. Bake in a hot oven and serve one pizza to each child. Or if you want to celebrate St Patrick's Day, make a green pizza. Use the basic dough and a thin layer of tomato, 42 g ($1\frac{1}{2}$ oz) mozzarella, spinach leaves, peas if liked, chopped fresh green pepper and green olives. Add 14 g ($\frac{1}{2}$ oz) of green food colouring to the dough or cook the spinach first, reserve the water and add some of that to the dough to colour it. For May Day add red pimentoes, sliced radishes and sweet corn to the tomato, and for St George's Day make a red cross across the pizza and put ricotta cheese with freshly-milled black pepper in the 4 sections.

To complete your party fare, serve side-dishes, salads and sweets as you think necessary. The following suggestions are particularly complementary to pizza, and are as well-suited to a meal for two as a party for twenty.

Antipasto

If you're having a pizza as a main course, together with a salad and perhaps a dessert to follow, you don't really need to serve anything to precede the pizza. That said, however, there are a few antipasto which work particularly well if you want to provide three courses. If you're feeling extravagant, serve melon halves filled with port or, to be more economical, slice the melon and sprinkle ginger on the slices. An avocado half covered with Italian salad dressing (page 90) is tasty and not too filling. Should you wish to serve something that's light and different, thinly slice some Hungarian gyula sausage, arrange the slices on plates for individual servings and add strips of red or green pepper and some olives to each serving. It's a good idea to provide cocktail sticks for the olives, and an ashtray for the olive stones and discarded sticks.

There are several dishes which are traditionally Italian. Of these, I think Tonno e Fagioli and Mozzarella and Tomato Salad are the best choices before a pizza.

Tonno e Fagioli (Tuna and Bean Salad)

84 g (3 oz) tuna
1 small onion
112 g (4 oz) beans (Italian cannellini or white butter beans)
3 black olives
oil, salt, pepper

Flake the tuna into small pieces. Thinly slice the onion and drain and rinse the beans. Cover the tuna with the onion rings, beans and black olives. Sprinkle with oil, add salt and freshly-milled black pepper and serve. You can also add capers and anchovy fillets, split, but it's not advisable if you're using either of these ingredients in your pizza.
Serves 2

Mozzarella and Tomato Salad

This is known as 'Mozzarella Cosa Nostra' at one of my favourite haunts, the Factotum. It is a popular and delightful salad, and is also good as a side dish or, in larger quantities, as a main course. To serve it as antipasto, you will need 112 g (4 oz) mozzarella and 2 tomatoes for every two people. Slice the cheese, salt lightly and cover with a generous amount of freshly-milled black pepper. Slice the tomatoes, season with salt and pepper, and arrange the tomato slices around the mozzarella. Add some crushed fresh basil and a generous sprinkling of oil, garnish with olives or slices of green pepper, and serve with rolls made from reserved pizza dough (allow about 14 g (½ oz) dough per roll). French dressing or wine vinegar can enhance the tomato, but if you use it be sure that it doesn't run on to the cheese.

Salads

As pizzas are exotic and flavoursome you can afford to keep the salad simple. It must be well chilled and served on equally cool plates. A crispy cos lettuce, washed, well dried, and broken into bite-sized pieces, plus a radish or two, sliced cucumber, spring onions and a few tomato wedges make an ideal salad. Rub the bowl in which you will toss the salad with a skinned garlic clove. The dressing is of course very important; the recipe below will keep for weeks in a refrigerator.

Italian Salad Dressing

1 egg yolk or white
1 teaspoon sugar
1 teaspoon salt
pinch black pepper
1 teaspoon French or German mustard
1 teaspoon brandy
¼ teaspoon Worcestershire sauce
1.5 dl (¼ pint) olive, soya or maize oil
0.75 dl (⅛ pint) wine vinegar
oregano
parsley

Beat the egg yolk until creamy, or the egg white until stiff. Add the sugar, salt, pepper, mustard, brandy and Worcestershire sauce and beat until the mixture thickens. Add the oil, slowly at first, then more rapidly. Add the vinegar, then more sugar or salt to taste if needed. If the dressing is greasy but has a strong vinegary taste, mix in a little lemon juice; if it is too thick and will not pour easily, simply add some water. Stir in a little oregano and some chopped fresh parsley.

This dressing will make a fine Cole Slaw when used to bind finely shredded white cabbage, grated carrot and green pepper.

Caesar Salad

I like the story of how the Caesar Salad was created. A Mexican hotelier called Caesar was overwhelmed by a sudden rush of guests who almost ate him out of house and home. The guests kept arriving and he was left with nothing but lettuce, eggs and some stale bread. He told his staff to use their showmanship and present the newly christened Caesar Salad with such a display of pageantry that customers would believe it was the speciality of the house. This new salad was born with the sort of panache that befits a pizza.

1 cos lettuce
2 or 3 cloves garlic
oil for frying
4 slices bread, cubed
1 egg
1 tablespoon wine vinegar
3 tablespoon olive oil
dash Worcestershire sauce
4 anchovy fillets
1 teaspoon salt
pinch black pepper
7 g (¼ oz) Parmesan

Break the lettuce into bite-sized pieces. Carefully wash and dry it. Chop the garlic and fry in oil until light brown, strain and discard the garlic. Fry the bread cubes in the garlic oil until golden brown. Drain off surplus oil.

Beat the egg, add the vinegar, olive oil and Worcestershire sauce, and continue beating lightly. Pound the anchovies and stir into the mixture. Tip the mixture on to the lettuce, season, and toss gently. Remove from bowl and place the salad on chilled plates. Toss croûtons in salad bowl, then add them to the salad. Sprinkle lightly with Parmesan.
Serves 4

Garlic Bread

Though it may seem too heavy a combination, garlic or herb bread is very popular with pizza addicts as an accompaniment to the meal. You can make the bread by using surplus pizza dough, shaped into a long roll and baked at 220°C (425°F)/Gas 7 for 15 minutes. Otherwise use French bread or a chubby roll.

1 loaf bread
1 clove garlic (or more to taste)
112 g (4 oz) soft butter

Chop or grind the cleaned garlic. Mix with the butter until the smell of garlic suits you. Make four or five diagonal cuts in the loaf and paint the garlic butter into the cuts. Brush the top of the loaf with a little melted butter. Place on a baking tin used only for this purpose (otherwise you might one day be serving garlic meringues) or wrap the loaf in aluminium foil and place on a rack in the oven. Bake in a hot oven for about 3 minutes or until the garlic butter has melted into the surrounding bread. Serve hot.

For herb bread follow the same principle, making a strong herb butter from chopped parsley and chives, thyme and parsley, sage, savory and parsley, or tarragon and chives.

Sweets

Fresh fruit salad follows a pizza perfectly. The following recipe is simple to make, but if you are looking for a dish which takes even less time try adding wine or liqueur to almost any fruit. Marsala, red or white wine can be poured over strawberries, raspberries, or sliced fresh peaches. Kirsch or tequila sharpens up the flavour of fresh pineapple. I am a great experimenter with wines and spirits poured over fruit and find them much less cloying than the never-ending cream.

Fruit Salad

For a really good fruit salad it is essential to use fresh fruit. A shot of Maraschino can be added to this recipe to give it an extra lift. The quantities of water, sugar and lemon juice given here are those necessary for fruit for 4 servings.

3 dl (½ pint) water
112 g (4 oz) sugar
½ lemon
Fresh fruit as available :
  orange, apple, grapefruit,
  pear, melon, pineapple,
  plums, grapes, bananas,
  peaches

Dissolve the sugar in the water by whisking it with a fork. Squeeze in the juice of half a lemon.

Cut the fruit into thin slices, trying to maintain the recognisable shape of the fruit. Apples and pears may be peeled or not, according to preference; if you don't peel them, be sure to slice them very thinly.

Peel the oranges and grapefruits with a sharp knife. Then, holding the fruit over the bowl, cut out segments with a knife, as you would when preparing a grapefruit, leaving no pith or skin on the oranges or grapefruits. Tangerines are not so successful in fruit salads because they are less easy to skin.

The fruit salad should be well cooled in the refrigerator before serving. Do not add sliced bananas until shortly before you serve the salad or they will become mushy.

Rhubarb and Orange Sorbet

A cool, tangy sorbet will follow a spicy pizza perfectly. Here is a recipe kindly given to me by that master of water ices from Haverstock Hill, Anacleto Mansi of Marine Ices. Have long Russian cigarettes, the real ones with a hollow tube at one end, available to offer your guests as the sorbet is served. This will complete your meal in style!

1 small tin rhubarb
56 g (2 oz) lump sugar
3 small oranges, peeled
168 g (6 oz) granulated
  sugar
3 dl (½ pint) water
2 egg whites

Place the rhubarb and its juice in an electric liquidiser or blender, adding some of the water if necessary. Rub the lump sugar on the rind of the orange to absorb the zesty fragrant oils of the orange peel, then place the lumps of sugar in the rhubarb mixture. Dissolve half the granulated sugar in the remainder of the water, squeeze the oranges and add the juice.

Combine the two liquids and mix well, then put in a pre-chilled basin and place in the freezing compartment of a refrigerator for about 4 hours, stirring occasionally.

When the mixture appears to have solidified, beat very vigorously for two to three minutes. In a small bowl, beat the egg whites with the remainder of the granulated sugar until they are stiff and fluffy. Lightly fold the egg whites into the mixture and return to the freezing compartment until required.
Serves 3–4

93

Syllabub

A fifteenth-century recipe, this was a favourite at the banquets of Henry VIII where it helped to cleanse the mouth after a surfeit of chicken legs.

2 fresh egg whites
112 g (4 oz) white sugar,
  granulated or caster
juice of half a good lemon
140 g (5 oz) sweet white wine
280 g (10 oz) double or
  whipping cream

Beat the egg whites until they are very stiff, then beat in the sugar, the lemon juice and the wine. Beat the cream fairly stiff. *Fold* the cream into the previous mixture; do not beat at this stage. Spoon the syllabub into 3 or 4 champagne glasses or ice-cream cups and freeze for a couple of hours before serving.

This curious concoction will be stiff until you add the wine, when all will turn sloppy. On the addition of the thick cream, however, the syllabub will become even thicker than it was before.

You can keep this dessert almost indefinitely while it's frozen; once thawed, however, it should be eaten within a couple of hours or it will separate and the wine will fall to the bottom.

Zabaglione

A light and delicious sweet after a pizza, this frothy combination originates from the Saracens, Sicily, or the home of pizza itself—Naples. In southern Italy it is often served with a knowing wink, to fortify newlyweds.

Use one egg yolk per person, plus one over (e.g. 4 egg yolks for three people). Beat the eggs well in a pyrex bowl if you do not have the special rounded-bottom copper saucepan which Italian chefs use.

Add a half eggshell of caster or granulated sugar for each egg and continue beating the eggs to a thick cream until you cannot hear the sugar grind in the mixing bowl. *Fold* in a half eggshell of Marsala for each egg used, adding a dash of dry white wine to the Marsala each time. It's very important to fold this in rather than beat it; otherwise you will lose the valuable air bubbles you have introduced into the mixture.

Place the bowl in a saucepan of simmering water, and beat hard around and across the zabaglione. A whisk is ideal for this. When the mixture expands and thickens and starts to curl away from the side of the bowl, stop whisking and pour into pre-warmed glasses. Serve zabaglione immediately with a cat's tongue biscuit or a light sponge finger.

A light dash of cinnamon enhances this gorgeous dessert. Zabaglione may also be served chilled.

Table of Wines

Ai Funghi: Birra Peroni
American: Californian dry white, or Coca Cola
American Hot: Cold Schlitz beer
Aries: Rosé de Provence
Aquarius: St Emilion
Calzone: Barbera (dry red)
Cancer: Worthington E
Capricciosa: Baresco (full-bodied red)
Capricorn: Champagne
Chicago: Beaujolais Village (dry red)
Chinese: Jasmin tea
Cockney Pride: Merrydown cider
Colonel's: Cabernet d'Anjou
Con Cozze e Vongole: Gewürztraminer (dry white)
Connoisseur: Vodka from ice-coated bottle
Fiorentina: Verdicchio (dry white)
Four Cheeses: Barolo (full-bodied red)
Four Seasons: Orvieto secco (dry red)
Francoforte: Moselle or Hock (medium-dry white)
Gemini: Pouilly Fuissé (well-chilled)
Giardiniera: Hock (medium-dry white)
Inglese: Double Diamond
King Edward's: Guinness
La Reine: Claret (dry)
Leo: Mersault (dry white)
Libra: Montrachet (dry white)
Margherita: Chianti Classico (red)
Maria Stuarda: Chablis
Marinara: Chianti
Michelle: Spanish dry white

Monica: Mateus (rosé)
Mushroom: Frascati secco (dry white)
Napoletana: Ravello, Gran Caruso (dry white)
Neptune: Lacrima Christi Del Vesuvio (dry white)
Olympico: Demestica (white)
Onion and Anchovy: Valpolicella
Parmentier: Chianti
Pietro: Vino Bianco Toscano (medium-dry white)
Pisces: Frascati
Prawn: Soave (dry white, chilled)
Saggitarius: Bloody Mary
San Terenzio: Soave (dry white)
Scorpio: Gattinara (*chambré*) or similar such as Ghemme, Spanna or Sizzano
Siciliana: Corvo Salaparuta (dry red or white)
Sloppy Giuseppe: Rioja (red)
Taurus: St Emilion (*chambré*)
Vegetarian: iced lemon tea
Veneziana: Merlot (dry red)
Vesuvio: Lacrima Christi
Virgo: Meursault (chilled)
Whitebait: Adgestone (dry white English, chilled)

Index

Note: Recipes are listed in italic. Where a pizza is referred to in more than one place, the page on which you will find the recipe is noted in bold. The round-up of Italian pizzas (pages 81–4) is not included in the index.